Ephesians
The Treasures of Family

Ephesians
The Treasures of Family

By

Dr. Bo Wagner

Word of His Mouth Publishers
Mooresboro, NC

All Scripture quotations are taken from the **King James Version** of the Bible.

ISBN: 978-1-941039-38-0
Printed in the United States of America
©2023 Dr. Bo Wagner

Word of His Mouth Publishers
Mooresboro, NC
www.wordofhismouth.com

All rights reserved. No part of this publication may be reproduced in any form without the prior written permission of the publisher except for quotations in printed reviews.

Table of Contents

	Introduction to Ephesians	7
1	Accepted in the Beloved	9
2	It's All Good	23
3	The Happiest of Prayers	33
4	It's Great to Be Alive	43
5	Grace for the Gentiles	53
6	Of Rubble and Riches	61
7	The Messenger to the Messy	69
8	The Fellowship of the Mystery	77
9	It's Worth It All	87
10	A Worthy Walk	95
11	Gifts for the Body	103
12	Being Gentile is Okay: Being Like Other Gentiles Is Not Okay	127
13	As Becometh Saints	143
14	As Different as Day and Night	155
15	Of Submission and Spirit Filling	165
16	The Model Marriage	173
17	Obedience and Gentleness	189
18	Armor Up	201
19	No Time for Timidity	213
	Works Cited	219
	Other Books by Dr. Bo Wagner	221

Introduction to Ephesians

Like the book of Galatians, Paul was not writing at random when he penned this letter to the Ephesians. He had something in mind. And that something was the fact that God had chosen to bring Gentiles into the family of God on an equal plane with believing Jews. He expressed that purpose very clearly in the second chapter of this epistle:

Ephesians 2:11 *Wherefore remember, that ye being in time past Gentiles in the flesh, who are called Uncircumcision by that which is called the Circumcision in the flesh made by hands;* **12** *That at that time ye were without Christ, being aliens from the commonwealth of Israel, and strangers from the covenants of promise, having no hope, and without God in the world:* **13** *But now in Christ Jesus ye who sometimes were far off are made nigh by the blood of Christ.* **14** *For he is our peace, who hath made both one, and hath broken down the middle wall of partition between us;* **15** *Having abolished in his flesh the enmity, even the law of commandments contained in ordinances; for to make in himself of twain one new man, so making peace;* **16** *And that he might reconcile both unto God in one body by the cross, having slain the enmity thereby:* **17** *And came and preached peace to you which were afar off, and to them that were nigh.* **18** *For through him we both have access by one Spirit unto the Father.* **19** *Now therefore ye are no more strangers and foreigners, but fellowcitizens with the saints, and of the household of God;*

This was an absolutely radical concept and one that often got Paul into a great deal of trouble. In fact, it ultimately led to his death.

But we all owe him a great deal of gratitude for not just telling that truth everywhere he went but also writing that truth here in the Epistle to the Ephesians. If there is ever any book that we believers in the Gentile world ought to cling to with utter gratefulness, the book of Ephesians is it.

So let's jump in.

Chapter One

Accepted in the Beloved

Ephesians 1:1 *Paul, an apostle of Jesus Christ by the will of God, to the saints which are at Ephesus, and to the faithful in Christ Jesus:* **2** *Grace be to you, and peace, from God our Father, and from the Lord Jesus Christ.* **3** *Blessed be the God and Father of our Lord Jesus Christ, who hath blessed us with all spiritual blessings in heavenly places in Christ:* **4** *According as he hath chosen us in him before the foundation of the world, that we should be holy and without blame before him in love:* **5** *Having predestinated us unto the adoption of children by Jesus Christ to himself, according to the good pleasure of his will,* **6** *To the praise of the glory of his grace, wherein he hath made us accepted in the beloved.*

Those last four words, even if you do not fully understand them yet, have a beauty and power that is evident to anyone. No one wants to be rejected, especially by anyone important to them. And believers in Christ, no matter where they came from, no matter their background, aren't. We are accepted in the beloved. All of these first six verses will build to that glorious crescendo.

A focused delivery

Ephesians 1:1 *Paul, an apostle of Jesus Christ by the will of God, to the saints which are at Ephesus, and to the faithful in Christ Jesus:*

It was somewhere around A.D. 63 that Paul penned this epistle to the Ephesians. Many of the things said in this book, along with the following three passages, very clearly lead us to believe that he was under house arrest in Rome when he did so:

Ephesians 3:1 *For this cause I Paul, the prisoner of Jesus Christ for you Gentiles,*

Ephesians 3:13 *Wherefore I desire that ye faint not at my tribulations for you, which is your glory.*

Ephesians 6:20 *For which I am an ambassador in bonds: that therein I may speak boldly, as I ought to speak.*

So, Paul did not have very long to live when he wrote this letter. That would have been the case even if he was not heading for the chopping block; he was already referring to himself as "Paul the aged:"

Philemon 1:9 *Yet for love's sake I rather beseech thee, being such an one as Paul the aged, and now also a prisoner of Jesus Christ.*

So this great man, who had given so much for the cause of Christ and who had preached and written about so many vital topics of Scripture, chose in the last days of his life to write an incredible discourse on the Gentiles and full salvation. It was obviously incredibly important to him, or he would never have wasted the short yet valuable time that he had left to do so.

And when he wrote this letter, he had some very specific people in mind to receive it and read it. Look at verse one again:

Ephesians 1:1 *Paul, an apostle of Jesus Christ by the will of God, to the saints which are at Ephesus, and to <u>the faithful in Christ Jesus</u>:*

The first group of people for whom Paul intended this focused delivery was the saints which are at Ephesus, the believers in Christ who lived there. And it is little wonder that Paul wrote and directed this, one of the most glorious portions of Scripture, to that group of people; he had invested a great deal in them already.

Let's go back and see where it all began because this will help you to understand Paul's heartbeat for these people.

Acts 18:18 *And Paul after this tarried there yet a good while, and then took his leave of the brethren, and sailed thence into Syria, and with him Priscilla and Aquila; having shorn his head in Cenchrea: for he had a vow.* **19** *And he came to Ephesus, and left them there: but he himself entered into the synagogue,* *and reasoned with the Jews.* **20** *When they desired him to tarry longer time with them, he consented not;* **21** *But bade them farewell, saying, I must by all means keep this feast that cometh in Jerusalem: but I will return again unto you, if God will. And he sailed from Ephesus.*

Paul was on his second missionary journey. It was on this particular journey that he took the gospel to a place that we now know by a very familiar name: Europe. This was really the main start of the Gentile world hearing about Christ and that He loved them and wanted to save them.

In Acts 18, he was wrapping up this second missionary journey and was currently on his way back to Jerusalem. And for a very brief time, he stopped in over at Ephesus. Naturally, as he most always did, he went into the synagogue and told the Jews about Jesus, their Messiah. They wanted him to stay around longer and tell them more, but he was really set on getting to Jerusalem for the feast (most likely the Passover) to worship.

And that very clearly provided a "torn betwixt and between" situation for Paul. Here was an open door for the gospel, but he really wanted to get to Jerusalem to worship at the feast.

It appears that Paul was only there for one Sabbath day, then he left. But he did leave Priscilla and Aquila there to continue the work. And while they were there, Apollos showed up preaching about the baptism of John. Priscilla and Aquila told him the things he did not know about Jesus, and he clearly received their instruction.

On his third missionary journey, Paul came through Ephesus again, and this time, he devoted much more time to the people in that city:

Acts 19:8 *And he went into the synagogue, and spake boldly for the space of three months, disputing and persuading the things concerning the kingdom of God.* **9** *But when divers were hardened, and believed not, but spake evil of that way before the multitude, he departed from them, and separated the disciples, disputing daily in the school of one Tyrannus.*

As you can see, his first three months there were spent in the synagogue, once again trying primarily to reach the Jews. But for the most part, that met with nothing but opposition. So

Paul stopped going to the synagogue, and he and his few converts went to a school run by a man named Tyrannus.

Adam Clarke said,

> "It appears that the person in question was a schoolmaster and that he lent or hired his room to the apostles; and that they preached daily in it to as many, both Jews and Gentiles, as chose to attend. It is very likely that Tyrannus was a Jew, and was at least well affected to the Christian cause; for we have many proofs that individuals among them kept schools for the instruction of their youth; besides the schools or academies kept by the more celebrated rabbins. The school of Tyrannus might have been such a place as Exeter Hall, and such like places for public and especially for extraordinary religious meetings in London." (6:842)

Trying to give the gospel in the synagogue met with very little success and a whole lot of opposition. But "moving the meeting to a new location," as we would put it in our modern terminology, ended up succeeding wildly:

Acts 19:10 *And this continued by the space of two years; so that all they which dwelt in Asia heard the word of the Lord Jesus, <u>both Jews and Greeks</u>.*

We are talking about millions of people who heard the gospel while Paul was there in Ephesus the second time around. He preached, and people went everywhere talking about it and telling what he was saying. And people, including very notable sinners, started getting born again and proving it by open confession and repentance of sin:

Acts 19:18 *And many that believed came, and confessed, and shewed their deeds.* **19** *Many of them also which used curious arts brought their books together, and burned them before all men: and they counted the price of them, and found it fifty thousand pieces of silver.* **20** *So mightily grew the word of God and prevailed.*

This was a huge, visible, incredible moving of God. This was not just the typical shallow emotional "God accepts you just the way you are" excuse for revival and/or evangelism we see so often today. This was a genuine work of God, with the genuine proof of confession and repentance and forsaking of sin. And, as will most often be the case with that type of the moving of God, the backlash was severe.

The center of wealth creation in Ephesus was the temple of the pagan goddess Diana. It was one of the wonders of the ancient world. But when so many people started getting saved and forsaking that paganism, that cash cow started drying up. And when cash cows start drying up, the people who own the cash cows get very angry.

A man named Demetrius, one of the silversmiths who made and sold miniature silver shrines of that temple, gathered everyone together and started a mob riot designed to destroy Paul and Christianity and restore their cash cow to its former profitable glory.

Paul ended up having to leave town. According to Acts 20:31, he was there, in total, for approximately three years; yet now he had to leave. He was not in the habit of spending anywhere near that amount of time in any one location; usually, it was far less. But he knew that Ephesus was the center of paganism in the world of that day and that if a church could survive and thrive there, that church could change the world. He likely would have stayed even longer for that purpose but ended up having to leave, doubtless with a bit of a broken heart.

But he left a church behind. A very good church. And, as you would fully expect from a city like Ephesus, it was a mixed church, a church made up of both Jews and Gentiles, though predominantly Gentile. Remember, his first converts there were those that he won to Christ from right out of the synagogue. And yet, as he penned chapter two of this epistle, he is addressing the church as Gentiles. So again, it is abundantly clear that this church had some Jews and even more Gentiles in it. And apparently, at some point, that started causing some problems, problems that led Paul to write this amazing book.

So again, Paul's focused delivery in this book was first of all to the saints at Ephesus, both Jew and Gentile.

But under the inspiration of God, it also was focused on a wider audience. Look at verse one again:

Ephesians 1:1 *Paul, an apostle of Jesus Christ by the will of God, to the saints which are at Ephesus, <u>and to the faithful in Christ Jesus:</u>*

That last phrase expands the audience greatly. In other words, the truths that we see expressed in the book of Ephesians apply to believers everywhere. They were written first and foremost to the believers in Ephesus, but they were also written to all the rest of us. And that is very good since most of us are Gentiles and thus very much in need of the premise and the promise of this book.

A fond desire

Ephesians 1:2 *Grace be to you, and peace, from God our Father, and from the Lord Jesus Christ.*

Before we get into the doctrinal details of this verse, we should take just a moment to point out something more practical about this verse. From time to time, you will meet people who are very ignorant or very dishonest who proclaim that Paul probably did not write the letter to the Ephesians. This despite the fact that the very first verse of the letter literally says, *"Paul, an apostle of Jesus Christ by the will of God, to the saints which are at Ephesus."*

For normal people, that kind of thing is what you call "a clue."

But, ignoring that clue and ignoring all of the other clues, like the fact that he was right then in chains of bondage, they proceed further to say weird and vaguely intellectual sounding things like, "The writing and tone of this letter do not seem to match the writing and tone of Paul's other letters, so he probably didn't write it."

It is almost like they never even get around to reading past the very first verse of this epistle because if they ever made it to the second verse, they may actually notice something:

Ephesians 1:2 *Grace be to you, and peace, from God our Father, and from the Lord Jesus Christ.*

Romans 1:7 *To all that be in Rome, beloved of God, called to be saints: Grace to you and peace from God our Father, and the Lord Jesus Christ.*

1 Corinthians 1:3 *Grace be unto you, and peace, from God our Father, and from the Lord Jesus Christ.*

2 Corinthians 1:2 *Grace be to you and peace from God our Father, and from the Lord Jesus Christ.*

Galatians 1:3 *Grace be to you and peace from God the Father, and from our Lord Jesus Christ,*

Philippians 1:2 *Grace be unto you, and peace, from God our Father, and from the Lord Jesus Christ.*

Colossians 1:2 *To the saints and faithful brethren in Christ which are at Colosse: Grace be unto you, and peace, from God our Father and the Lord Jesus Christ.*

2 Thessalonians 1:2 *Grace unto you, and peace, from God our Father and the Lord Jesus Christ.*

Letter after letter after letter after letter, Paul used this same phrase. And yet the skeptical doctors and doctorettes of the law who do not have the least bit of confidence in God or in Scripture flip their bright pink hair away from their glasses and say, "The wording in Ephesians doesn't sound like the writings of Paul."

People of this ilk could hear the phrase, "And now you know the rest of the story," and say, "That doesn't sound at all like something Paul Harvey would say."

But back to the doctrinal content of this verse, Paul fondly desired that the Ephesian believers be granted grace and peace from God the Father and from the Lord Jesus Christ.

He knew, of course, that all the world is the recipient of the general grace of God that brings salvation down to mankind:

Titus 2:11 *For the grace of God that bringeth salvation hath appeared to all men,*

He also clearly knew that the Ephesians had personally, individually received the saving grace of God:

Ephesians 2:8 *For by grace are ye saved through faith; and that not of yourselves: it is the gift of God:* **9** *Not of works, lest any man should boast.*

What he was desiring for them, and for us, therefore, in verse one, was the daily grace of God, God continuing to give them all the good things day by day that they needed but did not deserve.

As to the peace that he desired for them, and for us, that was obviously not the being brought into peace with God in salvation that he wrote of in Colossians 1:20 since, again, they already had that. Just as with grace, this was a daily peace that he was wishing for them and for us, peace that transcends our circumstances. Here is how he expressed it when he wrote to the Philippian church:

Philippians 4:7 *And the peace of God, which passeth all understanding, shall keep your hearts and minds through Christ Jesus.*

From those fond desires, it is very clear that Paul dearly loved the saints in Ephesus and all the faithful in Christ Jesus.

A foundational declaration

Ephesians 1:3 *Blessed be the God and Father of our Lord Jesus Christ, who hath blessed us with all spiritual blessings in heavenly places in Christ:* **4** *According as he hath chosen us in him before the foundation of the world, that we should be holy and without blame before him in love:* **5** *Having predestinated us unto the adoption of children by Jesus Christ to himself, according to the good pleasure of his will,* **6** *To the praise of the glory of his grace, wherein he hath made us accepted in the beloved.*

If you paid careful attention as you read through those four verses, you likely noticed that they make up one very long sentence. And this one very long sentence in these four verses makes up a foundational declaration for what Paul will cover in this epistle.

Ephesians 1:3 *Blessed be the God and Father of our Lord Jesus Christ, who hath blessed us with all spiritual blessings in heavenly places in Christ:*

One of the most important words in this verse is also one of the smallest words, the little three-letter word "all." God the Father has blessed us with ALL spiritual blessings in heavenly places in Christ.

This really is key to the epistle. Paul was going to spend several chapters teaching the saved Gentiles that they were on an equal plane with saved Jews. And he began here to lay the foundation for that by telling them that God does not grant them part of His blessings since they are *just Gentiles*; He grants them all of His blessings since they are *in Christ*!

You Gentile believers may as well stop looking jealously at Jews and even Jewish believers and feeling that you are somehow inferior; anyone in Christ is the recipient of all of His blessings that apply to the saved. And do not let that reference to heaven in this verse fool you into thinking that all these blessings are yet to come, and we will be granted them when we get to glory. Notice carefully that it does not say "in heaven," it says, "in heavenly places."

So even here on earth, anywhere we go that has become a heavenly place because of the presence of Christ is a place that we are recipients of His full blessings to the saved.

Ephesians 1:4 *According as he hath chosen us in him before the foundation of the world, that we should be holy and without blame before him in love:*

As we make our way into verse four, we are entering verses that have become a needless battlefield through the years because of a very wrong view of God and Scripture and a removal of these verses from their overall context.

The wrong view of God that I am referring to is the view held by Calvinism and Calvinists, commonly these days referred to by the term reformed theology. Very simply put, their view is that before time itself, God chose who was going to go to heaven and who was going to go to hell, and then He created them for that purpose and to that end. That, of course, is not the accurate, clearly stated view of God that Scripture presents:

2 Peter 3:9 *The Lord is not slack concerning his promise, as some men count slackness; but is longsuffering to us-ward, <u>not willing that any should perish, but that all should come to repentance.</u>*

The God of Scripture does not want anyone to die and go to hell, and He has not elected or predetermined anyone to do so.

The wrong view of Scripture that I spoke of a moment ago is also the view held by Calvinism, and it is the view that certain Scriptures Lord over all other Scriptures and all of the other Scriptures must be made to fit within those select few, no matter how one has to squeeze and crush and distort them to make them do so.

Passages from Romans 9 are a prime example of this. If that or any other passage were a sole cornerstone passage of Scripture by which all others must be measured, then one could find justification for doing damage to other Scriptures to make them fit. But no Scripture rules all other Scripture. The proper view of Scripture is that all of it must reconcile since all of it is God-breathed:

2 Timothy 3:16 *All scripture is given by inspiration of God...*

Every passage that vaguely sounds like man does not have a choice in his own salvation must be balanced and reconciled with the myriad of passages that clearly proclaim that he does have a choice in his own salvation.

So as we begin verse four and read the words, *"According as he hath chosen us in him before the foundation of the world, that we should be holy and without blame before him in love,"* let me tell you plainly that neither this verse nor any verse that follows teaches what reformed theology claims that they teach. John Wesley thought so as well, commenting on this verse, "Both Jews and Gentiles, whom he foreknew as believing in Christ." (Linder)

He was correct. But taking it a step further, please remember, this entire book is written not as a treatise on salvation, though much doctrine of salvation is given within it, but to help Jews and Gentiles realize that they are to be an undivided family in Christ. And that is why, while Paul himself was a Jew, he wrote to a mixed audience of mostly Gentiles in Ephesus and used the word "us" in this verse.

So Paul was saying, "Before there was time, before there was an earth, before there were Jews, before there were Gentiles, God chose us, Jews and Gentiles both, to be holy and without blame before him in love." Paul knew that God's design in saving people was not to have one group of saved people be holy and the other "only sort of holy since they came from a bad background;" it was His desire for all the saved to be completely holy, not just positionally, but even practically. He also knew that it was God's desire for everyone, no matter their background, to be *"without blame before him in love."*

This phrase is also incredibly important to understand in the light of what Paul was trying to accomplish in this epistle. It was not God's desire just that both Jew and Gentile be absolutely holy both in position and in practice. It was also His desire that both Jew and Gentile be without blame before God when it comes to love.

Throughout the New Testament, the Jews and Gentiles constantly had strife between themselves that had to be dealt with. And it wasn't right. It wasn't supposed to be. Nor is it supposed to be the case in our day.

You and I can dress like we live in the "Little House on the Prairie." We can go to church every time the doors are open. We can throw our televisions out in the yard and shoot them with shotguns. We can fast three days out of the week. We can tithe ninety percent instead of ten percent. We can live like the Amish. We can sing only out of the "red back hymnal." And yet, if we do not behave in love towards each other, God is not satisfied in the least.

Some of the most outwardly "holy acting" people I have ever known have also been some of the most caustic and condescending and downright hateful people I have ever known.

That is not what God designed us for, it is not what He predestined us to when He called us, and it is not what He expects of us. We are to be holy, and we are to be blameless in this matter of love.

Ephesians 1:5 *Having predestinated us unto the adoption of children by Jesus Christ to himself, according to the good pleasure of his will,*

Verse five gives us the next incredible thing that God has predestined both Jews and Gentile believers to be part of, namely the adoption of children.

The Family Bible Notes gives one of the most accurate definitions of the word adoption, and it is absolutely beautiful. It says that it means to "pass from the condition and spirit of servants to the privileges and filial spirit of sons, in a state not of minority and servitude, but of manhood and freedom." (Linder)

In other words, when we think of adoption, we only think of it in the way our Western minds know it. We think of it as a baby or young child simply being brought into a family. But in Bible terms, it meant much more than that. It meant to be brought into a family and then to be elevated to the status of a fully blessed adult within that family. So when Paul told a mixed audience of Jews and Gentiles that God had predestined them to this adoption, he was once again dealing not with salvation but with the blessings that come from salvation. He was once again telling them that no matter where they came from, no matter their background, the moment they got saved, God regarded all of them as top-level in His family. It wasn't a situation where the Jews who got saved started off way up near the top of the ladder and only had one or two rungs until they got to the very top when it came to blessings, but the Gentiles who got saved started off way at of the bottom of the ladder (which was probably propped up on defiled dirt right nearby the Temple of Diana they had once worshiped at) and had a lot further to go. No, both Jew and Gentile, when they get saved, are immediately elevated to equal status as full-grown children of God when it comes to the blessings of salvation.

We may not even be full-grown as humans yet, but as far as status in God's family goes, the only thing that matters is whether or not we have received Christ. If we have, all of the blessings of believers, all of the privileges of being in God's family, equally belong to all of us, Jew or Gentile.

You say, "But they may not be worthy of that!"

It is almost certain that that is exactly how the Jews felt about their Gentile brothers and sisters in Christ. And that is why the last half of verse five is so powerful and important:

Ephesians 1:5 *Having predestinated us unto the adoption of children <u>by Jesus Christ to himself, according to the good pleasure of his will,</u>*

May I make those words very simple to you? This thing of God granting equal status and blessings both to Jews and Gentiles who believe is the way it is because Jesus Christ Himself likes it that way. It is His idea. And all of it is designed to serve a purpose, a purpose that Paul clearly states in the next verse:

Ephesians 1:6 *To the praise of the glory of his grace, wherein he hath made us accepted in the beloved.*

When we believing Gentiles realize the grace that God has given us in this, when we understand that Christ did not come through us, and the Scriptures did not come through us, and that our kind spent thousands of years rejecting God, and yet He has given us all of this anyway, we ought to praise the glory of His grace over and over and over again. And we ought to do so, not so much for all the blessings, but as the last half of this verse says, because that grace has made us "accepted in the beloved." That word accepted comes from the word *karitos,* and it means, among other things, "highly favored," or in our vernacular, something like "adored."

We should have been rejected by the beloved, meaning by the Son. We should have been cast into hell by the beloved. We should have had the beloved say to us, "Depart from me, you who have no rights in the commonwealth of Israel."

But instead, we have been fully accepted, not just *by* the Beloved, but *in* the Beloved.

In verse one, He called us "the faithful **in** Christ Jesus."

In verse three, He said that He has "blessed us with all spiritual blessings in heavenly places **in** Christ."

In verse four, He says, "he hath chosen us **in** him."

We believing Gentiles are not on the periphery of this thing called the family of God: we are **in Christ**, we are fully, thoroughly, completely in the family just as much as any Jew who has ever believed.

We are *Accepted in the Beloved.*

Chapter Two

It's All Good

Ephesians 1:7 *In whom we have redemption through his blood, the forgiveness of sins, according to the riches of his grace;* **8** *Wherein he hath abounded toward us in all wisdom and prudence;* **9** *Having made known unto us the mystery of his will, according to his good pleasure which he hath purposed in himself:* **10** *That in the dispensation of the fulness of times he might gather together in one all things in Christ, both which are in heaven, and which are on earth; even in him:* **11** *In whom also we have obtained an inheritance, being predestinated according to the purpose of him who worketh all things after the counsel of his own will:* **12** *That we should be to the praise of his glory, who first trusted in Christ.* **13** *In whom ye also trusted, after that ye heard the word of truth, the gospel of your salvation: in whom also after that ye believed, ye were sealed with that holy Spirit of promise,* **14** *Which is the earnest of our inheritance until the redemption of the purchased possession, unto the praise of his glory.*

As we ended our first section of verses at verse six, we saw Paul reminding his Gentile converts that we are not just tolerated by the Beloved; we are accepted in the Beloved! And it is that Beloved, Christ, that is still on his mind as he begins verse seven with the words *"in whom."* And he is going to go on from there to tell us just how good it is that that Whom, Jesus, has brought us to Himself. This will be eight verses where everything is literally all good.

The grace is all good

Ephesians 1:7 *In whom we have redemption through his blood, the forgiveness of sins, according to the riches of his grace;* **8** *Wherein he hath abounded toward us in all wisdom and prudence;*

As Paul begins, he uses two very good words of blessing and a very good word of basis. The blessing words are redemption and forgiveness. Redemption is from the word *apolutrosin*, and it means "a release from captivity, a paying of one's ransom." Forgiveness is from the word *aphesin,* and it means "the cancellation of sin and a release of prisoners."

This is what we equally receive when we get saved, whether Jew or Gentile. Our "Whom," our Beloved, Christ Jesus, paid our ransom by His own blood and death, releases us from our captivity, cancels our sin, and makes us no longer prisoners.

That really is all good! All of that represents absolute salvation; there is nothing left to be done, ever.

But it is that basis word, grace, that lets us know why we can have those blessing words, redemption and forgiveness. As Paul will make very clear in the next chapter, salvation does not come by our works; it always and only comes by God's grace. Grace, here, is from the word *xaritos,* and as always, it means "a free gift, something we do nothing to deserve."

Verse eight starts with the word "wherein," which goes right back to that word grace. God has abounded in grace toward us in all wisdom and prudence. In other words, when God lavishes this grace on us, though it may seem foolish to the devil, to the world, and even to the Jews, it is actually a manifestation of the wisdom and prudence of God. God did not "make a mistake" when He predestined the Gentiles to be brought into the family of God; everything He ever does is wise and prudent, including this.

Honestly, there are times that even I, a part of the Gentile world, look at the Gentile world and think, "God, are you really sure you want any of us? Because from what I can see, that sure doesn't seem like a very good choice."

But God, in His wisdom and prudence that is far too high and holy for me to ever fully comprehend, has chosen to lavish His saving grace on the putrid Gentile world just as much as on the pedigreed Jewish world.

The gathering is all good

Ephesians 1:9 *Having made known unto us the mystery of his will, according to his good pleasure which he hath purposed in himself:* **10** *That in the dispensation of the fulness of times he might gather together in one all things in Christ, both which are in heaven, and which are on earth; even in him:*

It is in these verses that Paul begins to broach the overall subject of the letter. Mind you, he has already been talking about it for eight verses now, but here is where he will begin to make that clear to his readers when he starts talking about God "gathering" some things.

In verse nine, Paul tells his readers that God has "*made known unto us the mystery of his will.*" When you see that word mystery, which comes from the word *mustayrion*, it means "a secret, something that had previously been hidden to some degree."

Now, please understand how much of a giant shockwave that word sent through the Jewish world of Paul's day. They did not think for one second that anything concerning God's dealings in salvation was hidden or mysterious at all. They believed that God loved Jews and despised the Gentiles; nothing mysterious at all about that. So when Paul, in the context of salvation, writing mostly to Gentiles, said in so many words, "Here's something about salvation that not many people know," that was a really shocking statement.

But there was a mystery of salvation that not many people, especially the Jews, knew. Mind you; they could have known since the Old Testament did make reference to it in many places, places like this:

Isaiah 49:6 *And he said, It is a light thing that thou shouldest be my servant to raise up the tribes of Jacob, and to restore the preserved of Israel: I will also give thee for a light to* *the Gentiles, that thou mayest be my salvation unto the end of the earth.*

So Paul, who himself had somehow ignored this passage and many others, had finally been brought to the place where he understood the mystery of God's will when it comes to salvation, namely that the Gentiles would be included. And this was not a distasteful thing to God; verse nine says that it was and is *"according to his good pleasure which he hath purposed in himself."*

This matter of the Gentiles being granted access to salvation is something that very much pleased God. And He did not have to take a poll or convene a council on it; He simply purposed it in Himself. The pure and holy God, the almighty Creator of the universe, purposed to bring Jews and Gentiles both into the family of salvation.

The sentence is still going, so look at how the thought continues in verse ten:

Ephesians 1:10 *That in the dispensation of the fulness of times he might gather together in one all things in Christ, both which are in heaven, and which are on earth; even in him:*

A word is introduced here that is only used four times in Scripture, all in the writings of Paul, the word *dispensation.* In all four usages of this word, it comes from the word *oikonomia,* and we get our word *economy* from it. It means "management, administration, and stewardship." Adam Clarke defines it this way, "a plan for the management of any sort of business." (6:433) And that is indeed a good way to summarize its meaning, especially here.

Another phrase we need to look at before we begin to discern the meaning of the entire verse is the phrase *"the fulness of times."* You quite likely recognize that from another famous New Testament passage:

Galatians 4:4 *But when the fulness of the time was come, God sent forth his Son, made of a woman, made under the law,* **5** *To redeem them that were under the law, that we might receive the adoption of sons.*

In Ephesians 1 the fullness of the time is from *playromatos tone kairone,* and in Galatians 4 it is from the very similar *playroma tou kronou.* In both cases, it refers to God's final stage in dealing with man about salvation. You see, prior to the coming of Christ, man's knowledge of salvation was incomplete, not full. But Christ was the revelation of all that the Old Testament had alluded to. He ushered in the era of full knowledge of salvation and made it available to all to understand.

So when you put all of that together, verse ten is God's way of saying that in this New Testament era, or economy, as it is often called based on that word dispensation, it is God's pleasure to *"gather together in one all things in Christ, both which are in heaven, and which are on earth; even in him."*

This, as I have already said, begins to go to the heart of the book. The "all things in Christ" includes those who are in Christ because they are recipients of His salvation, and that includes both Jews and Gentiles. It is God's plan to gather them together in heaven, but also to gather them together here on earth!

If we are honest, there are a lot of people that we dislike for one reason or another, of whom we think, "We will wait until we get to heaven, and we will be okay together there." There were likely some Jews that were willing to be at least that "generous" to Gentiles.

But that is nowhere near good enough to God. The God who gave everything to save both Jews and Gentiles expects both Jews and Gentiles to be gathered as one here and now on earth, not just when we get to heaven. Put in modern terms, God is not interested in "Christian segregation." He does not put together Jewish churches or Gentile churches or black churches or white churches or brown churches or red churches; He just puts together blood-bought churches.

And we Gentiles ought to regard that as very good indeed because we were the ones who, in Paul's day, were generally on the outside looking in.

The glory is all good

Ephesians 1:11 *In whom also we have obtained an inheritance, being predestinated according to the purpose of him who worketh all things after the counsel of his own will:* **12**

That we should be to the praise of his glory, who first trusted in Christ.

Verse twelve ends the very long sentence that began way back in verse seven; Paul would not have been a favorite of modern grammar teachers.

The "in whom" that Paul begins verse eleven with refers back to Christ in verse ten. In Christ, we, the saved, have obtained an inheritance.

Paul seems to have loved this word; he used it once when writing to the church at Galatia, four times when writing to the church here at Ephesus, and once when writing to the church at Colosse. And in every case, it means exactly what we think of when we use the word inheritance in our modern day.

This inheritance that Paul references at the beginning of verse eleven is spelled out for us in the rest of verse eleven and verse twelve:

Ephesians 1:11b ...*being predestinated according to the purpose of him who worketh all things after the counsel of his own will:* **12** *That we should be to the praise of his glory, who first trusted in Christ.*

Our inheritance is that we should be to the praise of His glory. In other words, our inheritance is that God would save us and then transform us from the dirty, broken creatures that we were into clean, whole, holy Children of God that cause God to be glorified when we are looked at. And, as the first part of verse eleven states yet again, none of this was an afterthought, even for the Gentiles. God predestined all of this after the counsel of His own will. It was His choice, His idea. The world may not like it, the devil definitely does not like it, many Jews despised it, but God did it because He liked it.

Before we move on, look at verse twelve again, and let me show you one more significant thing:

Ephesians 1:12 *That we should be to the praise of his glory, who first trusted in Christ.*

Who is it that is going to end up being "*to the praise of His glory*"? Those who "*first trusted in Christ.*"

That sounds pretty important, doesn't it? But what does it mean? Is it talking about first as in "before somebody else?" Certainly not. It does not matter when you get saved, only *that* you get saved. Those two words, "first trusted," come from the word *proaylpikotis*. It means "to hope before." In other words, to put your faith in Christ and to be saved as a result of that. One comes before the other. It did even in Abraham's time:

Romans 4:3 *For what saith the scripture? Abraham believed God, and it was counted unto him for righteousness.*

Galatians 3:6 *Even as Abraham believed God, and it was accounted to him for righteousness.*

This shows our responsibility in salvation, and believe me, we do have one. Salvation is not a situation where we are walking along in our lostness, and God, without warning or call, yanks us into "savedness." Salvation is an offer, not a deed done to us. It is by grace; it is a gift.

But back to the main thought of these verses, our salvation and the change that comes from it is to the praise of His glory. God so changes us that when God or angels or even sensible people see us, they want to glorify the God who made the difference in our lives.

The gospel is all good

Ephesians 1:13 *In whom ye also trusted, after that ye heard the word of truth, the gospel of your salvation...*

If you are paying attention, you cannot help but notice all of these "in whoms." And just like the previous ones, this one also refers back to Christ.

Notice the progression given here, a progression that once again shows our responsibility in salvation and what happens in what order. We place our trust in Christ after we hear the word of truth. God sends the message, and then we are responsible for responding to it. We are responsible for trusting what we have heard.

And what message have we Gentiles heard along with the Jews? The gospel, meaning the good news of our salvation.

Gospel is a distinctly New Testament word; it is used one hundred one times in the Bible, all of them from Matthew to Revelation.

Adam Clarke once again gets the understanding of this verse right, saying:

> "Ye Gentiles, having heard from us the word, the doctrine of the truth, which is the Gospel, or glad tidings, of your salvation, have believed, as we Jews have done, and received similar blessings to those with which God has favoured us." (6:434)

It really is very good news that God did not leave mankind to die in his sin. It is very good news that He brought the gospel first to the Jews, His people. It is also very good news that He did not stop there and also brought it to us Gentiles.

There is absolutely nothing bad in this; it really is all good!

The guarantee is all good

> **Ephesians 1:13b** ...*in whom also after that ye believed, ye were sealed with that holy Spirit of promise,* **14** *Which is the earnest of our inheritance until the redemption of the purchased possession, unto the praise of his glory.*

Yet again, we find an "in whom," and yet again, it refers back to Christ. And, yet again, we find a chronology of salvation given here. We believe, and then after we believe, we are sealed with the Holy Spirit of promise.

This chronology that is repeatedly given in these verses is very important because from time to time, you will encounter people who sound very eloquent as they say very wrong things. They will say that God saves us, and *then* we put our faith in the One who saved us. They will say that because we were dead in trespasses and sin, we could not place any faith in Christ; He had to save us and make us alive first so that we could place our faith in Him.

But in order to believe that, you must first of all either ignore or explain away multiple passages just like this one that says, "***after*** *that ye believed, ye were sealed with that holy Spirit of promise*" and "*That we should be to the praise of his glory, who* ***first trusted*** *in Christ*," and then you must also ignore all of the Scriptural examples of those who believed and then received salvation and the Holy Spirit.

With that understanding, look at these verses again with me and notice the guarantee that is given to us when we get saved:

Ephesians 1:13b *...in whom also after that ye believed, ye were sealed with that holy Spirit of promise,* **14** *Which is the earnest of our inheritance until the redemption of the purchased possession, unto the praise of his glory.*

You may well remember another place where the sealing of the Spirit is mentioned. It is also right here in the letter to the church at Ephesus:

Ephesians 4:30 *And grieve not the holy Spirit of God, whereby ye are sealed unto the day of redemption.*

In both of these passages, the word sealed is from *esphragisthayta* and means "to seal, to secure, to affirm." It was the picture of a legal document being sent from one person to another, with the signet seal of the sender affixed to the letter. Throughout the Bible, we see that practice, most notably perhaps in the days of Esther and Ahasuerus and also in the days of Darius and Daniel.

In theological terms, the moment we believed in Christ, the Holy Spirit became God's seal on us. From that very moment, we were forever affirmed as His, we were absolutely secure, and our seal is not temporary under any circumstances; it is all the way until the day of redemption.

Here, again, is how verse fourteen put that part for us:

Ephesians 1:14 *Which is the earnest of our inheritance until the redemption of the purchased possession, unto the praise of his glory.*

Most of you have heard of "earnest money." In our vernacular, it is a down payment, a guarantee that all of the rest will be coming. When we got saved, we did not immediately get all of our inheritance as Children of God. I live in a house not a mansion, my street is asphalt not gold, and if I do not pay the power bill, I will be living in the dark.

But what we did get as a guarantee of all that we will get is the "down payment" of the Holy Ghost of God, both living inside of us (1 Corinthians 6:19-20) and sealing us until the day of redemption. And look one last time at how the end of verse fourteen describes that:

...until the redemption of the purchased possession, unto the praise of his glory.

This "redemption" is very clearly different from the redemption mentioned in verse seven. The redemption in verse seven dealt with God bringing us into His family at salvation; it was the redemption of our soul and spirit. This redemption deals with the same thing that Paul spoke of in Romans 8:23:

Romans 8:23 *And not only they, but ourselves also, which have the firstfruits of the Spirit, even we ourselves groan within ourselves, waiting for the adoption, to wit, the* ***redemption of our body.***

Notice that in both of these verses, Paul mentions the Holy Spirit being given to us as an earnest/firstfruit, and in both verses, he mentions the redemption that we are waiting for.

God has already purchased us, as verse fourteen says. That redemption is done. But we still have so much more "redemption" to come! One day, our bodies will be as perfect and sinless as our spirit and soul, again to the praise of His glory, not ours. But until then, even on the days that we struggle so badly that we have a hard time believing it, we have the Holy Spirit inside us as a down payment, a guarantee that it is all going to happen.

The grace is all good, the gathering is all good, the glory is all good, the gospel is all good, the guarantee is all good; everything about salvation really is all good!

Chapter Three

The Happiest of Prayers

Ephesians 1:15 *Wherefore I also, after I heard of your faith in the Lord Jesus, and love unto all the saints,* **16** *Cease not to give thanks for you, making mention of you in my prayers;* **17** *That the God of our Lord Jesus Christ, the Father of glory, may give unto you the spirit of wisdom and revelation in the knowledge of him:* **18** *The eyes of your understanding being enlightened; that ye may know what is the hope of his calling, and what the riches of the glory of his inheritance in the saints,* **19** *And what is the exceeding greatness of his power to us-ward who believe, according to the working of his mighty power,* **20** *Which he wrought in Christ, when he raised him from the dead, and set him at his own right hand in the heavenly places,* **21** *Far above all principality, and power, and might, and dominion, and every name that is named, not only in this world, but also in that which is to come:* **22** *And hath put all things under his feet, and gave him to be the head over all things to the church,* **23** *Which is his body, the fulness of him that filleth all in all.*

These verses are both a prayer and praise all at once, and they are some of the most joyful verses in the entire Bible. They are also nine verses that make up one very long sentence. Once again, Paul would not be a favorite of any modern grammar teachers but should certainly be a favorite of anyone who understands how gracious God has been to us!

A reason for thanks

Ephesians 1:15 *Wherefore I also, after I heard of your faith in the Lord Jesus, and love unto all the saints,* **16** *Cease not to give thanks for you, making mention of you in my prayers;*

Communication in our day really is a very convenient thing. If you want to speak to someone half a world away, you can do so in under ten seconds' time with just the push of a few buttons. You can even face time them and see them while you are speaking to them! But in Paul's day, that was clearly not the case. As such, Paul's tearful goodbye to the Ephesian elders in Acts 20 was very probably the last time he ever spoke to any of them.

Thus, years have passed by, and Paul finds himself in Rome on trial for his life with not much longer to live. And yet, happily, someone brings him word of how those he loved in Ephesus are doing, and it was a really encouraging message. Paul heard of their *"faith in the Lord Jesus, and love unto all the saints."*

How blessed must it have been for him to hear that the Ephesians were still right on both sides of the coin? Many claim to have strong faith in Jesus and yet have no love for the saints. Others claim to love the saints but have no true faith at all in Christ, at least not the real one, the one the Bible describes for us. But the Ephesians were not deficient in either; their faith was right, and their fellowship was right.

Because of this, Paul was able to say that I *"Cease not to give thanks for you, making mention of you in my prayers;"*

Take that very literally. Every time Paul thought of them, his automatic attitude was one of thanks, and he was regularly praying over them because of how grateful he was for them.

Think about that. Generally, when someone is being prayed for constantly, it is because of something that is wrong. As you read this, you likely have people on your heart that you love who are lost. You pray for them constantly because you are brokenhearted at the thought of them dying and going to hell. You likely also have friends or family members who are in severe physical distress, perhaps even battling a life-threatening illness. You pray for them constantly because you want them to get better.

You may also be, like so many others these days, in great financial distress. You pray constantly because the bills are coming due, and you need God to step in and meet the need.

Or perhaps you simply have children who are wayward and wandering away from God and into the paths of sin. You are much like the father of the prodigal son no doubt was, constantly praying for your erring child to get right and come home.

But Paul prayed for the Ephesians constantly, not because anything was wrong, but because so much was right!

That should be our goal concerning others' prayers for us!

A request for growth

Ephesians 1:17 *That the God of our Lord Jesus Christ, the Father of glory, may give unto you the spirit of wisdom and revelation in the knowledge of him:* **18** *The eyes of your understanding being enlightened; that ye may know what is the hope of his calling, and what the riches of the glory of his inheritance in the saints,* **19** *And what is the exceeding greatness of his power to us-ward who believe, according to the working of his mighty power,*

As Paul begins to give more of the content of his happy prayer in verse seventeen, he also ends up giving us a bit of theology proper, meaning theology specifically centered on God Himself. He mentions *"the God of our Lord Jesus Christ, the Father of glory."*

This is obviously both a partial reference to the Trinity and also a reminder of the structure and nature of God. God the Father and God the Son and God the Holy Spirit all make up the One God. But God the Father is the authoritative head of the Godhead. He is *"the God of our Lord Jesus Christ."* Even Jesus acknowledged Him as such on multiple occasions:

Matthew 27:46 *And about the ninth hour Jesus cried with a loud voice, saying, Eli, Eli, lama sabachthani? that is to say, My God, my God, why hast thou forsaken me?*

John 20:17 *Jesus saith unto her, Touch me not; for I am not yet ascended to my Father: but go to my brethren, and say unto them, I ascend unto my Father, and your Father; and to my God, and your God.*

And yet, Christ Himself is also fully God:

Colossians 2:9 *For in him dwelleth all the fulness of the Godhead bodily.*

John 1:1 *In the beginning was the Word, and the Word was with God, and the Word was God.* **2** *The same was in the beginning with God.* **3** *All things were made by him; and without him was not any thing made that was made.*

Hebrews 1:8 *But unto the Son he saith, Thy throne, O God, is for ever and ever: a sceptre of righteousness is the sceptre of thy kingdom.*

Clearly, then, God the Father is God and God the Son is God, but God the Son regards God the Father as His God. Mind you, this is not something that our finite minds can ever fully plumb the depths of, but it is something that we can believe based on God's revelation of it to us in His Word.

But back to the prayer, what exactly was it that Paul was asking God to do for his beloved Ephesians?

Here was his opening request:

That God "*may give unto you the spirit of wisdom and revelation in the knowledge of him*:"

What exactly does all of that mean?

The Geneva Bible notes very much captures the basic essence of these words, saying, "it is not enough for us to have known God once, but we must know him every day more and more." (Linder)

This is much what Paul meant when he said to the Philippians, "*That I may know him, and the power of his resurrection, and the fellowship of his sufferings, being made conformable unto his death.*" (**Philippians 3:10**)

But if we are to truly know Him, the two words that Paul uses about that knowledge will be crucial to that pursuit:

"The spirit of *wisdom* and *revelation*."

In inverse order, we can know God more fully each day by a spirit produced from revelation and wisdom. Revelation is what God has told us in His word; wisdom is what we derive from a proper study and application of that revelation. And both are gifts from God.

Paul was praying for more and more of this in the lives of the Ephesians, and we would do well to pray for and pursue more and more of it in our own lives as well.

Continuing in a logical progression from that, Paul went on to say this in verse eighteen:

Ephesians 1:18 *The eyes of your understanding being enlightened; that ye may know what is the hope of his calling, and what the riches of the glory of his inheritance in the saints,*

The knowledge of God that comes from revelation and wisdom needs a proper recipient for the revelation and wisdom that brings that knowledge, someone who has their spiritual eyes open. And it is, once again, God who does that "enlightening" of the eyes. And when He does, we are able to more fully know what the hope of His calling is and what the riches of the glory of His inheritance is.

So, what are those two things?

The hope of His calling is the hope that is sourced out of His calling. In other words, since He is the one who called us to salvation, we can have the unshakable expectation that our salvation will never falter or fail; it is secure because of its source. So many wrestle with the assurance of salvation, and often those wrestlings are born out of a misplaced view of source; we somehow think that it is our faith that sources our salvation rather than Christ, the object of our faith. Once we get to the place that we remember where, or Whom, rather, salvation comes from, it becomes a truly hopeful, joyful thing.

The riches of the glory of His inheritance in the saints is, in the words of Adam Clarke, "the glorious abundance of the spiritual things to which you are entitled, in consequence of being made children of God." (6:435) When we get saved, it is much more than a future ticket to heaven; it is a present fullness of life. Here is how Jesus put those two aspects:

John 10:10 *The thief cometh not, but for to steal, and to kill, and to destroy: I am come that they might have life* [future ticket to heaven], *and that they might have it more abundantly* [present fullness of life].

If you are waiting until you get to heaven to enjoy the blessings of being saved, you are behind on that joy by an entire lifetime!

The next thing Paul prayed for the believers in Ephesus to have knowledge of was this:

Ephesians 1:19 *And what is the exceeding greatness of his power to us-ward who believe, according to the working of his mighty power,*

For all that he has gotten right in this text thus far, Clarke misses this one pretty badly, saying, "the apostle is here speaking of the glorious state of believers after death, the exceeding greatness of his power, or that power which surpasses all difficulties, being itself omnipotent, is to be understood of that might which is to be exerted in raising the body at the last day." (6:435)

Just a look at the third word of this verse should suffice to show the error in this, the word "is." This power is not a "will be" item; it is an "already is" item. Barnes gets this one right saying:

> "He refers not merely to the power which he had evinced in their salvation, but also to what the gospel was able to accomplish, and which they might yet experience. The 'power' referred to here, as exercised towards believers, does not refer to one thing merely. It is the whole series of the acts of power towards Christians which results from the work of the Redeemer. There was power exerted in their conversion. There would be power exerted in keeping them. There would be power in raising them up from the dead, and exalting them with Christ to heaven. The religion which they professed was a religion of power. In all the forms and stages of it, the power of God was manifested towards them, and would be until they reached their final inheritance." (Linder)

Paul wanted the Ephesians to know that God's power was working in their lives for their good, every single moment of every single day.

Here is what you need to know about that: when we see God's power working in our lives, God's power is working in our lives, and when we do not see God's power working in our lives, God's power is working in our lives.

It is not according to our circumstances. As redundant as it sounds, Paul said that the exceeding greatness of His power is according to the working of His mighty power. And it only makes it more interesting to realize that those are two different words for power. The first one comes from the pretty well-known word *dunamis,* which Alfred Nobel used to coin our English word dynamite, but the second comes from the word *kratos,* meaning dominion. In other words, His raw power comes from His royal power. His power in our lives is a result of who He is.

A reminder of greatness

Ephesians 1:20 *Which he wrought in Christ, when he raised him from the dead, and set him at his own right hand in the heavenly places,* **21** *Far above all principality, and power, and might, and dominion, and every name that is named, not only in this world, but also in that which is to come:*

Verse twenty ties in with the last phrase of verse nineteen. Taken together, here is what you have:

Ephesians 1:19b *...according to the working of his mighty power,* **20** *Which he wrought in Christ, when he raised him from the dead, and set him at his own right hand in the heavenly places,*

It was God the Father's mighty power that He wrought in Christ. That word wrought is from the word *energeo;* we obviously get our word energy from it. God the Father's power was the energy that raised Christ from the dead and then lifted Him back up into heaven forty days later and set Him back on His right hand.

May I point out the obvious? We, mankind, could use every bit of our power, our energy, and never raise a single dead person back to life, let alone lift them into the throne room of heaven. Thus, this is a happy reminder of the greatness of God the Father. There truly is no God like our God!

But the greatness of God does not stop with the Father; it fully extends to the Son as well. Here is how Paul put it in verse twenty-one:

Ephesians 1:21 *Far above all principality, and power, and might, and dominion, and every name that is named, not only in this world, but also in that which is to come:*

When God the Father raised the Son out of the grave and then back into heaven, He raised Him above all principality, and power, and might, and dominion, and every name that is named, not only in this world, but also in that which is to come.

But He did not raise Him just above all principality, and power, and might, and dominion, and every name that is named, not only in this world, but also in that which is to come, He raised Him FAR above all principality, and power, and might, and dominion, and every name that is named, not only in this world, but also in that which is to come.

The first four words Paul uses here for what Jesus is above, principality and power and might and dominion, are four ways to describe authority. The first one is used to describe the origin of authority (*arkay*, beginning), the second one is used to describe the overarching of authority (*exousia*, power, the right to command), the third one is used to describe outworking of authority (*dunamis*, raw practical power) and the fourth one is used to describe the ownership of authority (*kuriotays*, lordship).

Whatever earth knows of those four dynamics of power, whatever the universe knows of those four dynamics of power, Jesus is above absolutely all of that. And this is the God that the Ephesians placed their trust in and that we have placed our trust in.

But Paul also says in this verse that Jesus is above *every name that is named.*

Names in this world are endued with power to one degree or another. For good or bad, there is power in names like Trump, Windsor, Musk, and Bush. Pick the most powerful name that you will, though, and Jesus is above that name in power.

But notice what the end of the verse says about that:

Ephesians 1:21 *Far above all principality, and power, and might, and dominion, and every name that is named, <u>not only in this world, but also in that which is to come:</u>*

There are two things you should pay attention to. One, the fact that Jesus will be above every name, even in the future world. And two, that there is a future world! The world that we now live in, the universe that we now inhabit, will burn up with a fervent heat, right down to the very elements. But God has promised a new heaven and a new earth, and this verse is a scriptural reference to that new heaven and new earth.

And in that new heaven and new earth, Jesus will still be the greatest one anywhere.

A recognition of station

Ephesians 1:22 *And hath put all things under his feet, and gave him to be the head over all things to the church,* **23** *Which is his body, the fulness of him that filleth all in all.*

He, the Father, has put all things under His, the Son's, feet. His station is that He is over all.

Here is how Paul put that when he was writing to the Colossians:

Colossians 1:16 *For by him were all things created, that are in heaven, and that are in earth, visible and invisible, whether they be thrones, or dominions, or principalities, or powers: all things were created by him, and for him:* **17** *And he is before all things, and by him all things consist.* **18** *And he is the head of the body, the church: who is the beginning, the firstborn from the dead; that in all things he might have the preeminence.*

But though Christ is over all things in general, both what Paul said here in Ephesians and also in the text we just read from Colossians give us a specific aspect of which He is unquestionably in charge:

Ephesians: *and gave him to be the head over all things to the church,*

Colossians: *And he is the head of the body, the church*

The culture does not get to be in charge of the church. Business does not get to be in charge of the church. Government does not get to be in charge of the church. Family does not get to be in charge of the church. The youth do not get to be in charge of the church. Christ is the head of the church, and therefore we look to His Word, the Bible, for the final word on every decision.

Dovetailing off of that truth, verse twenty-three goes on to say this:

Ephesians 1:23 *Which is his body, the fulness of him that filleth all in all.*

This verse refers to the church as his body, the body of Christ. That is a very common statement throughout the New Testament:

Romans 12:5 *So we, being many, are one body in Christ, and every one members one of another.*

1 Corinthians 12:27 *Now ye are the body of Christ, and members in particular.*

Paul wrote to multiple literal local churches and called them the body of Christ. That ought to tell you how important the church is to Him. Anyone minimizing the church is minimizing the body of Christ on earth, the very hands and feet that He presently uses to do His work among mankind.

Now look at the last half once more:

Ephesians 1:23 *Which is his body, the fulness of him that filleth all in all.*

In order to get at the entire truth of this verse, we should compare it to a sister verse from Colossians:

Colossians 2:9 *For in him* [Christ] *dwelleth all the fulness of the Godhead bodily.*

All three of the uses of fulness and filleth are from the same root word, *playraoh*. All of the fulness of the Godhead, the Trinity, dwells in Christ, who then fills all the world as the Godhead sees fit. And just like Christ is filled with the Godhead and thus is the fullness of the Father, the church, when it is doing Christ's bidding and empowered by Christ's Spirit, is filled with Christ and thus is the fullness of Christ. This means that as Christ was the body fully representing the Father on earth, the church is the body fully representing Christ on earth.

That is a huge responsibility. And we will likely never get it perfect.

But we should not be satisfied with anything less, and just the fact that He trusts us enough to put us in that position is a most glorious ending to *The Happiest of Prayers*.

Chapter Four

It's Great to Be Alive

Ephesians 2:1 And you hath he quickened, who were dead in trespasses and sins; 2 Wherein in time past ye walked according to the course of this world, according to the prince of the power of the air, the spirit that now worketh in the children of disobedience: 3 Among whom also we all had our conversation in times past in the lusts of our flesh, fulfilling the desires of the flesh and of the mind; and were by nature the children of wrath, even as others. 4 But God, who is rich in mercy, for his great love wherewith he loved us, 5 Even when we were dead in sins, hath quickened us together with Christ, (by grace ye are saved;) 6 And hath raised us up together, and made us sit together in heavenly places in Christ Jesus: 7 That in the ages to come he might shew the exceeding riches of his grace in his kindness toward us through Christ Jesus.

In the last section of verses we covered, Ephesians 1:15-23, we saw Paul writing the happiest of prayers. It was nine verses of Paul practically shouting for joy over what was going on in the lives of the Ephesians and how grateful he was for them. And now he will turn his attention to what seems like an odd matter – death. But oh, what life comes from it!

A living death

Ephesians 2:1 And you hath he quickened, who were dead in trespasses and sins; 2 Wherein in time past ye walked according to the course of this world, according to the prince of the power of the air, the spirit that now worketh in the children of disobedience:

In verse twenty of the previous chapter, the subject of death was introduced:

Ephesians 1:20 *Which he* [God the Father] *wrought in Christ, when he raised him from the dead, and set him at his own right hand in the heavenly places,*

This subject will continue on through verses five and six of chapter two:

Ephesians 2:5 *Even when we were dead in sins, hath quickened us together with Christ, (by grace ye are saved;)* **6** *And hath raised us up together, and made us sit together in heavenly places in Christ Jesus:*

So when we get into the very first verse of chapter two, we are in an entire section focused on the subject of death, a subject that Paul uses to point out an essential spiritual truth.

As verse one begins, we come to an important word that occurs five times in the New Testament, the word quickened.

Ephesians 2:1 *And you hath he* **quickened***, who were dead in trespasses and sins;*

This word is used as well in 1 Corinthians 15:36, Ephesians 2:5, Colossians 2:13, and 1 Peter 3:18. And in every single one of those verses, it is used as the opposite of the word die, dead, or death. And that is fitting since the word quickened comes from the root word *zoay*, meaning life; we get our English word zoology from it.

To be quickened means "to be brought to life." Just like God the Father brought the Son back to life as we saw in Ephesians 1:20, He, God the Father, has quickened, brought to life those who were dead in trespasses and sins, as Ephesians 2:1 says.

And yet, look at what verse two says:

Ephesians 2:2 *Wherein in time past ye walked according to the course of this world, according to the prince of the power of the air, the spirit that now worketh in the children of disobedience:*

The very first word of this verse, wherein, is pretty crucial to understand. It goes back to the phrase "dead in trespasses and sins" in verse one. In other words, in that state of death, in time past we walked according to the course of this world. The point is, the spiritual death we lived in was a very active thing.

When we think of death, activity is not at all what comes to mind! If we go to a funeral and are there mourning over the body, and suddenly there is a bunch of activity in the coffin, there are also going to be a bunch of people running screaming into the streets!

This is why I say that these two verses show us a living death. The word walk in this verse means "to walk, to progress, to make due use of opportunities." It is a very active thing. Sinners do not lay around doing nothing; they make sinful decisions every single day and then act on them. And the irony is that they think they are truly "living!" They think that we believers are the ones who are not really living life, and they are oblivious to the fact that they are as dead as dead can possibly be. In fact, it is far worse than they can even imagine. Paul said that they *"walked according to the course of this world, according to the prince of the power of the air, the spirit that now worketh in the children of disobedience."*

There are two things the dead sinner is following, usually without even realizing it. They are following the course of this world and the devil himself, here called *"the prince of the power of the air, the spirit that now worketh in the children of disobedience."*

The world is going to hell, the devil is going to hell, and the lost sinner is walking in the footsteps of both.

Adam Clarke explained it pretty powerfully and gave a great explanation of the word "course" as he did:

> "There is much force in these expressions; the Ephesians had not sinned casually, or now and then, but continually; it was their continual employment; they walked in trespasses and sins: and this was not a solitary case, all the nations of the earth acted in the same way; it was the course of this world, according to the life, mode of living, or successive ages of this world. The word *ayone*, the literal meaning of which is constant duration, is often applied to

things which have a complete course, as the Jewish dispensation, a particular government, and the term of human life; so, here, the whole of life is a tissue of sin, from the cradle to the grave; every human soul, unsaved by Jesus Christ, continues to transgress." (6:437)

This is the living death all sinners are bound in. And it is the devil's delight that they do so and that they stay that way. And he is not passive in the process. This passage calls him both the prince of the power of the air and the spirit that now worketh in the children of disobedience.

As the prince of the power of the air, he is often geographically hovering over the people of this world, observing all that they do. But as the spirit that is now working in the children of disobedience, he is also often right down where we live very personally and actively moving and motivating people to evil.

All of this is the living death that the Ephesians had been in before Paul won them to Christ, and all of it is the living death every one of us is in until someone wins us to Christ.

But I have obviously saved the good news of this verse for last: God the Father did not leave us in that horrible state of walking death. When the Ephesians got saved, they passed from death into life. When we got saved, we passed from death into life. Paul will say the same thing again in verse five; he really wanted to emphasize the fact that we are not what we once were. In the church to whom he was writing, a majority Gentile church, he wanted to remind them that they were not what they once were. God had so radically changed them, taking them from living death unto spiritual life, that they had every right to regard themselves as on an equal plane with any saved Jew.

Nor should any understanding believers among the Jews have objected to this; dead is dead no matter how good the body looks! Those Jews who had been dead in trespasses and sins may have made much more presentable corpses than the Gentiles who had been dead in trespasses and sins, but a corpse is still a corpse!

A likewise dilemma

Ephesians 2:3 *Among whom also we all had our conversation in times past in the lusts of our flesh, fulfilling the desires of the flesh and of the mind; and were by nature the children of wrath, even as others.*

The "among whom" of verse three refers back to the children of disobedience at the end of verse two. Paul told the Ephesian believers that "we all," meaning every believer, Jew or Gentile, used to live our lives as part of the children of disobedience, lives that were marked by the lusts of our flesh and the fulfilling of the desires of the flesh and of the mind.

Once again, Paul is going to pretty good lengths to remind these Gentile believers that they were equally as bad as Jewish sinners when they were lost and equally as redeemed as Jewish believers when they got saved.

This verse is also a very good insight into the nature of a sinner, a sinner of any racial background. A sinner's conversation, which is a word that means "their entire manner of life," is all about the lusts of the flesh and the fulfillment of the desires of the flesh and of the mind.

Simply put, before a sinner gets born again, he is not a good person. The world may view the sinner as a good person, family may view a sinner as a good person, but the best person the lost world has to offer is still going to be bound by the lusts of the flesh and the fulfilling of the desires of the flesh and of the mind.

Look at the last phrase of the verse, and you will once again see Paul emphasizing the equal station of Jews and Gentiles and once again explaining what their former sinful life was like:

...and were by nature the children of wrath, even as others.

Verse two referred to lost sinners as the children of disobedience. Verse three now refers to sinners as the children of wrath. Before getting saved, our spiritual DNA is a DNA of disobedience and wrath. We do not become sinners because we sin; we sin because we are sinners. We are disobedient and wrathful and a thousand other things that are abhorrent in God's sight.

But that very last simple-sounding phrase once again brings us back to the truth of our equal station:

...even as others.

This means, quite simply, "even as the rest of mankind is."

This dilemma of our living death is a likewise dilemma; everyone is born dead in trespasses and sins.

A lovely display

Ephesians 2:4 *But God, who is rich in mercy, for his great love wherewith he loved us,* **5** *Even when we were dead in sins, hath quickened us together with Christ, (by grace ye are saved;)* **6** *And hath raised us up together, and made us sit together in heavenly places in Christ Jesus:* **7** *That in the ages to come he might shew the exceeding riches of his grace in his kindness toward us through Christ Jesus.*

These are some of the most exquisite, precious, priceless verses in all of Scripture. Having just read the awful words, *"Wherein in time past ye walked according to the course of this world, according to the prince of the power of the air, the spirit that now worketh in the children of disobedience: Among whom also we all had our conversation in times past in the lusts of our flesh, fulfilling the desires of the flesh and of the mind; and were by nature the children of wrath, even as others,"* the next two words we come to are *"But God."*

Those are the two words that change everything.

The train of thought that begins with the words "But God" is this: But God, *even when we were dead in sins, hath quickened us together with Christ, and hath raised us up together, and made us sit together in heavenly places in Christ Jesus:*

But as you look at the verses in their entirety, you cannot help but be drawn to the box cars of treasure being pulled along with that train of thought. So, let's first of all look at the descriptive terms that make up those treasure cars, and then we will examine the main words of the thought itself.

Ephesians 2:4 *But God, <u>who is rich in mercy, for his great love wherewith he loved us,</u>*

After having read about our former life in sin, the living death that was marked by us being the children of disobedience and the children of wrath, after reading about the fact that we followed the course of this world and the devil himself, the prince of the power of the air, we cannot help but rightfully conclude that we are in desperate need of mercy above all else.

And God does not just grant us mercy; He is *rich* in mercy towards us. He does not sprinkle mercy on us; He lavishes mercy on us.

His mercy far exceeded our messy.

If our messy was somehow greater than His mercy, we would be in eternal trouble. But His mercy far exceeded our messy.

And this was for a reason. The last half of this verse says that it was *for his great love wherewith he loved us.* So, His mercy had a source, a fountainhead. The source of His mercy is His great love toward us. And understand that His love preceded His mercy which preceded our reception of it. He did not clean us up and then start loving us and then show mercy on us; He loved us when we were yet sinners and lavished mercy on us so that we could become saints.

And once again, these riches, both those that come before salvation and all that come after, are equal toward the Jew and the Gentile:

Romans 10:12 *For there is no difference between the Jew and the Greek: for the same Lord over all is rich unto all that call upon him.*

The next treasure phrase we find that adorns the main thought is the one in parenthesis *(by grace ye are saved;).*

He will say this again in verse eight. God lavishes His mercy on us and then saves us by His grace. He withholds from us the judgment that we do deserve and freely offers the salvation that we do not deserve.

Now look at the entire main thought again without the treasure words, the "does" without the "decoration."

But God... even when we were dead in sins, hath quickened us together with Christ... and hath raised us up together, and made us sit together in heavenly places in Christ Jesus:

Despite the fact that we were by nature the children of wrath and disobedience, despite the fact that we followed the course of this world and that of the prince of the power of the air, the devil himself, God, when we were dead in sins, has not just made us alive but has done so together with Christ.

What does it mean that He has quickened us together "with Christ?"

Barnes gives a good explanation of this:

"In connexion with him; or in virtue of his being raised up from the grave. The meaning is, that there was such a connexion between Christ and those whom the Father had given to him, that his resurrection from the grave involved their resurrection to spiritual life. It was like raising up the head and the members--the whole body together." (Linder)

Our resurrection and new life are inextricably tied to Christ's resurrection and new life. Ours was impossible without His. He went into death so that He could be raised so that we who were dead could also be raised. And once again, this is an "us" matter, meaning both Jews and Gentiles.

The last half of that verse is breathtaking:

...and made us sit together in heavenly places in Christ Jesus:

He has made us, both saved Jews and saved Gentiles, to sit together in heavenly places in Christ Jesus.

I have a question. Have you been to heaven?

Can you tell me what it is like?

But pay attention: this verse says that He "made us" to sit together in heavenly places in Christ Jesus. That is past tense in English, aorist tense in Greek, and both indicate something that has already happened. In fact, there is also an implied "hath" in this whole segment:

*But God, even when we were dead in sins, **hath** quickened us together with Christ, and **hath** raised us up together, and [**hath**] made us sit together in heavenly places in Christ Jesus:*

This is not exactly something we are waiting for. We are waiting for it, but it has also already happened.

Is your mind spinning yet?

It shouldn't be. The text of this epistle has already given you the explanation four times and will do so three more times before Paul rolls up this letter.

Ephesians 1:1 *Paul, an apostle of Jesus Christ by the will of God, to the saints which are at Ephesus, and to the faithful* **in Christ Jesus***:*

Ephesians 1:3 *Blessed be the God and Father of our Lord Jesus Christ, who hath blessed us with all spiritual blessings in heavenly places* **in Christ***:*

Ephesians 1:10 *That in the dispensation of the fulness of times he might gather together in one all things* **in Christ***...*

Ephesians 2:6 *And hath raised us up together, and made us sit together in heavenly places* **in Christ Jesus***:*

Here is another way that Paul said much the same thing:

Ephesians 1:22 *And hath put all things under his feet, and gave him to be the head over all things to the church,* **23** *Which is his body,* **the fulness of him** *that filleth all in all.*

The reason we have already been seated in heaven without even realizing it is because we are in Christ, we are His fullness, and He is already there!

Here is the entire list of all the ways that we can make that very simple and easy to fully understand:

-
-
-
-

There are none.

This is one of those "believe it, be amazed by it, but do not drive yourself crazy trying to figure it out" matters of Scripture. I cannot begin to give you a simple way of fully explaining how it is that since we are in Christ, we are already seated there in heaven while our body and soul and spirit are also still very much right here right now. I can just tell you that it is true; we are already seated together in heavenly places in Christ Jesus. And unlike the general heavenly places in Ephesians 1:3, this is very specifically heaven as well as we see both here and in Ephesians 1:20.

And it is important for you to know this for one very big reason: it is another reason why we believe in the doctrine of eternal security. You see, if we are already seated together in heavenly places in Christ Jesus, then for us to lose our salvation would mean that we were in heaven and then not in heaven. You will never find a verse of Scripture anywhere that gives credence to such nonsense!

All of this, by the way, has a very specific motive in the mind of God, and that motive is seen in the last verse in this section:

Ephesians 2:7 *That in the ages to come he might shew the exceeding riches of his grace in his kindness toward us through Christ Jesus.*

That, so that. The Father did all of this so that *in the ages to come he might shew the exceeding riches of his grace in his kindness toward us through Christ Jesus.*

God does what He does now so that He can show what He will show then.

God is holy and just and a million other impressive things. But He has done all of this, from making us, to coming down to earth for us, to dying for us, to raising from the dead for us, to saving us, so that He could have an entire rest of earthly time and then all of future eternity to showcase His grace through His kindness toward us through Christ Jesus.

All of our present days and then all of eternity is and will be about His grace. And that makes this entire "life" thing very, very enjoyable. If God did all of this just to find a way to forever demonstrate His wrath or His justice, we would be alive but wishing we were dead.

But since He has done all of this for the purpose of forever showcasing His grace, it really is good to be alive!

Chapter Five

Grace for the Gentiles

Ephesians 2:8 *For by grace are ye saved through faith; and that not of yourselves: it is the gift of God:* **9** *Not of works, lest any man should boast.* **10** *For we are his workmanship, created in Christ Jesus unto good works, which God hath before ordained that we should walk in them.* **11** *Wherefore remember, that ye being in time past Gentiles in the flesh, who are called Uncircumcision by that which is called the Circumcision in the flesh made by hands;* **12** *That at that time ye were without Christ, being aliens from the commonwealth of Israel, and strangers from the covenants of promise, having no hope, and without God in the world:* **13** *But now in Christ Jesus ye who sometimes were far off are made nigh by the blood of Christ.*

Most Christians know the first two verses of this section very well indeed. I would surmise that a healthy number of Christians actually have them memorized. And they should; these verses are foundational to our faith. They clearly lay out the truth that salvation is absolutely, completely of grace, with no works on humanity's part added in.

None of that is shocking to a Bible-believing Christian. But it becomes a bit shocking when you consider to whom these words were originally directed.

No works for the godless

Ephesians 2:8 *For by grace are ye saved through faith; and that not of yourselves: it is the gift of God:* **9** *Not of works, lest any man should boast.*

As I alluded to a few lines ago, there was an initial audience for the words of these verses. While they apply to absolutely everyone in the entire world without exception, the audience to whom they were first directed was a majority Gentile church. And here is why that is so important. As far as "relative goodness" goes, the Jews were far better than the Gentiles. The Jews had Abraham as their father while the Gentiles had no such spiritual giant as their federal head. The Jews had the rite of circumcision as a sign of their relationship with God while the Gentiles had nothing comparable. The Jews had the Old Testament Scriptures, sometimes called the oracles of God, while the Gentiles had nothing but vain pagan philosophy by way of a written guideline.

Because of all these advantages, the Jews were much more outwardly moral than the Gentiles. Mind you, Jesus pointed out that they were really whited sepulchers full of dead men's bones, but outwardly, they seemed to have all the advantages. Their behavior was much more what you would expect to see from "people of God."

So for the Jews to receive the message "there are no works that you can do to be saved; it is all of grace" would be a bit surprising. But for the Gentiles to receive the message "there are no works that you can do to be saved; it is all of grace" was absolutely shocking. If anyone needed to "be better," it was the Gentiles! If anyone needed to clean up their act, it was those pagans. If anyone needed to really strive to finally be clean, it was those dirty outcasts who had been wallowing in sin for countless generations.

So when God sent word that the Gentiles did not have to work for their salvation, when He sent word that their salvation would be entirely by grace apart from works, it was earth-shattering.

Again, please understand that these words apply to everyone, Jew and Gentile. But the fact that these words were sent specifically to a majority Gentile church is an excellent reminder of how foolish it is to trust in works for salvation. If God did not expect the filthy Gentiles to work for their salvation, then He does not expect anyone to work for their salvation.

As to the content of these two verses, it ties back to what came before in verse seven:

Ephesians 2:7 *That in the ages to come he might shew the exceeding riches of his grace in his kindness toward us through Christ Jesus.* **8** *For by grace are ye saved through faith; and that not of yourselves: it is the gift of God:* **9** *Not of works, lest any man should boast.*

For all of time and all eternity to come, everyone will be marveling about the riches of the grace of God through Christ Jesus because we are saved by grace through faith.

Those prepositions *by* and *through* teach us a few things about this. By means "on the basis of," and grammatically, this word grace ties directly back to the grace he mentioned in verse five. So understand it this way: by the grace, on the basis of this very grace, you are saved *through* faith.

Through is from the preposition *dia*, and it means "by means of." So the *by* gives the basis, and the *through* gives the means. Robertson's Word Pictures put it this way, "Grace is God's part, faith is ours." (Linder)

But then he adds another important phrase:

Ephesians 2:8 *For by grace are ye saved through faith; and <u>that not of yourselves</u>...*

As we get to that phrase, let me briefly make you aware that there is a bit of a controversy about what it is referring to. Some say that it refers to the grace and the faith; others say it refers directly back to the faith alone. Still others say that it refers to the "are ye saved" part since it is in the neuter gender, while both grace and faith are feminine in gender.

But that argument completely misses the obvious: the "are ye saved" part comes by, on the basis of grace, through, through means of faith. In other words, all three of them are inextricably tied together! So if you want to know which of these three things the "that" applies to, the answer is "yes!" It applies to all of them. The grace is not of ourselves, the faith is not of ourselves, and the salvation that comes on the basis of grace and through the means of faith is not of ourselves.

None of it is from us! The faith is our part as we have already said, that is certainly true. But even the faith that we act on comes from God. Simply put, God gives us the ability to believe, and then we choose whether or not we will. But if we do, if we exercise that faith that God has given us, and He applies the grace that He gives us, and it results in the salvation that He gives us, it is still all of Him.

Now look at the last part of verse eight and the thought that goes to the end of verse nine once again:

Ephesians 2:8 *For by grace are ye saved through faith; and that not of yourselves: <u>it is the gift of God:</u>* **9** <u>*Not of works, lest any man should boast*</u>.

That word "gift" is an absolutely beautiful word. It is from the word *doron,* and it means "a present," just like what we give each other at Christmas or on someone's birthday. This salvation that God offers us by grace through faith is a present, a good gift from His hands, something that we did not do anything to deserve, something that He offers us just because He loves us. And the reason He does it that way, according to verse nine, is so that it cannot be of works, and therefore no one can ever boast.

No one, absolutely no one ever works his way to heaven. No one gets saved by the work of baptism, or by the works of charity, or by the works of keeping the Ten Commandments, or by the works of confirmation, or by the works of praying the rosary, or by the works of doing two years of missionary service. No one ever gets saved by any works, period.

If they could, if they did, we would have to spend all of eternity listening to people crow about it. If salvation was by works, your neighbors in heaven would constantly be calling you like eternal extended car warranty salesmen to say, "We have been trying to reach you to tell you about the day that we worked our way into salvation!" But instead, since salvation is entirely by grace, since it is a gift, not something that we earn, we can all enjoy heaven as we glorify the God who gave us that good gift.

New workmanship for good

Ephesians 2:10 *For we are his workmanship, created in Christ Jesus unto good works, which God hath before ordained that we should walk in them.*

The "for" that begins verse ten ties back into the thought of verse nine:

Ephesians 2:9 *Not of works, lest any man should boast.* **10** *For we are his workmanship, created in Christ Jesus unto good works, which God hath before ordained that we should walk in them.*

Verse nine said, "not of works," and verse ten followed up on that with, "for we are his workmanship." In other words, it is an either/or proposition. Our salvation must either be of works, or we, the saved, must be His workmanship, His creation. It cannot be both. And since it cannot be by works, since that has been forcefully eliminated, we must therefore simply be His workmanship.

And yet, our works do have a role to play. That role is a post role rather than a pre role, though. We are not saved by works, we are instead His workmanship, but we, the saved, have been *created in Christ Jesus unto* [for the purpose of] *good works*.

We were created in Eden for good works: filling and tending to the earth.

We are created in Christ for good works as well.

Any being that God creates is for good works! We are not sparkles; we are servants. And this arrangement was not an afterthought:

Ephesians 2:10 *For we are his workmanship, created in Christ Jesus unto good works,* <u>*which God hath before ordained that we should walk in them.*</u>

Before, meaning before there ever was an us or a universe in which there could be an us, God had already preordained that we, the saved, whether Jew or Gentile, should be doing good works. Christ Himself taught this very plainly:

Matthew 5:16 *Let your light so shine before men, that they may see your good works, and glorify your Father which is in heaven.*

A believer who is not doing good works is not a Christian. A Christian is not just a believer but a believer who is behaving like Christ. As His workmanship, we are to be doing His works.

Putting the whole thought together, we are not saved by works, but as His workmanship, we are to be doing His works.

Not a way for the Gentiles

Ephesians 2:11 *Wherefore remember, that ye being in time past Gentiles in the flesh, who are called Uncircumcision by that which is called the Circumcision in the flesh made by hands;* **12** *That at that time ye were without Christ, being aliens from the commonwealth of Israel, and strangers from the covenants of promise, having no hope, and without God in the world:*

Paul now really begins to focus in on the saved Gentiles. He says, "Wherefore, because of the fact that you are created unto good works, remember some things."

What did Paul want them to remember because of the fact that they were created unto good works? He wanted them to remember where God brought them from. You see, doing the good works that God asks of us as believers is not always a pleasant thing. In fact, sometimes is a very unpleasant thing. But when we remember where God brought us from, we should be more than willing to behave as He asks.

Look at how far afield the Gentiles were before God extended salvation to them.

They were first of all "the uncircumcised." He said, "that is what you are called by that which is called the circumcision in the flesh made by hands," meaning the Jews. He differentiates here between the physical circumcision that the Jews so highly prized and the actual spiritual circumcision that God so highly prizes. But this rite that the Jews enjoyed as God's people was not something that the Gentiles were in the habit of practicing. And in the Old Testament economy, any man who was not circumcised was cut off from God.

He goes on to say, *"That at that time ye were without Christ, being aliens from the commonwealth of Israel, and strangers from the covenants of promise, having no hope, and without God in the world."*

There are five things he lays out here, each one of which was a spiritual nail in the coffin.

He says that they were without Christ, meaning that the Gentiles had no promised Messiah. He said that they were aliens from the commonwealth of Israel, meaning that they had no right whatsoever to the civil and religious privileges of the Jews. He said that they were "strangers from the covenants of promise," meaning that God made His promises to Abraham and his descendants, not to any of the Gentiles. He said that they had no hope, and they didn't, just empty lives followed by a brutal eternity. He said that they were without God in the world, and they were since they worshiped things of stone and wood made by their own hands.

Simply put, in that situation, there was not a "way" for the Gentiles. They merely wandered from one sin to another and from one false belief to another, none of which led them to the saving knowledge of God, and all of which left them in miserable bondage in this life.

But again, his point in reminding them of all of this was not to make them gloomy; it was to make them grateful! Since God reached far enough down to reach them in that putrid wallow of sin and darkness, they should be willing to be God's workmanship unto good works gladly, joyfully, enthusiastically. Those who have much from which they were rescued should have much good work to show their gratitude for that rescue.

Now welcomed by God

Ephesians 2:13 *But now in Christ Jesus ye who sometimes were far off are made nigh by the blood of Christ.*

This verse really begins the most glorious section of the book of Ephesians.

Paul set the table for this sweet feast with the bitter course that came before it. The Gentiles were without Christ, aliens from the commonwealth of Israel, strangers from the covenants of promise, people with no hope, and without God in the world.

They *were*.

But now...

Now *in Christ Jesus ye who sometimes were far off are made nigh by the blood of Christ.*

Sometimes means "formerly, in earlier times." The Gentiles used to be very far off from God; Paul just got done covering that with the mention of the five reasons that there was no way for them. But now, since Christ came and shed His blood for all, and since Paul had brought them the gospel of grace, and since they received that grace through their faith, now they were made nigh, meaning near. In other words, they were now welcomed by God. And not welcomed on a lesser plane than believing Jews, but on the exact same plane. Since salvation is by grace apart from works, none of what they used to be mattered against them, nor did any of what the Jews had always been matter for them!

God gave grace to the Jews who did not think they needed it – and He gave that exact same grace in the exact same measure to the Gentiles whom everyone knew needed it.

God gave grace to the Gentiles:

Us.

Chapter Six

Of Rubble and Riches

Ephesians 2:14 *For he is our peace, who hath made both one, and hath broken down the middle wall of partition between us;* **15** *Having abolished in his flesh the enmity, even the law of commandments contained in ordinances; for to make in himself of twain one new man, so making peace;* **16** *And that he might reconcile both unto God in one body by the cross, having slain the enmity thereby:* **17** *And came and preached peace to you which were afar off, and to them that were nigh.* **18** *For through him we both have access by one Spirit unto the Father.* **19** *Now therefore ye are no more strangers and foreigners, but fellowcitizens with the saints, and of the household of God;* **20** *And are built upon the foundation of the apostles and prophets, Jesus Christ himself being the chief corner stone;* **21** *In whom all the building fitly framed together groweth unto an holy temple in the Lord:* **22** *In whom ye also are builded together for an habitation of God through the Spirit.*

Paul spent his early life as an ultra-zealous Jew with absolute disdain for the Gentiles. And yet, when God saved him, He so changed his way of thinking that Paul became the greatest asset to the Gentile world. And he was determined to have everyone know that saved Gentiles were not just allowed in the family of God; they were adored in the family of God. So much so, that God did some very serious demolition work just for them.

A grand wreckage

Ephesians 2:14 *For he is our peace, who hath made both one, and hath broken down the middle wall of partition between us;* **15** *Having abolished in his flesh the enmity, even the law of commandments contained in ordinances; for to make in himself of twain one new man, so making peace;* **16** *And that he might reconcile both unto God in one body by the cross, having slain the enmity thereby:*

There is no question who the "he" is in this verse since the previous verse spelled it out for us not once, but twice:

Ephesians 2:13 *But now in* **Christ Jesus** *ye who sometimes were far off are made nigh by the blood of* **Christ***.*

This "He," our Lord Jesus Christ, is our peace, according to the first few words of verse fourteen. And the "our" means "we believers, both Jew and Gentile," as the rest of these verses make abundantly clear.

Look at all of verse fourteen again, and let me specify the details and identities.

Ephesians 2:14 *For he* [Christ] *is our* [both Jew and Gentile believers] *peace, who hath made both* [Jew and Gentile believers] *one, and hath broken down the middle wall of partition between us* [Jew and Gentile believers]*;*

This verse is both a cause of remembrance and rejoicing. On the remembrance side, it calls to mind the fact that there was once a "middle wall of partition" between Jews and Gentiles. This was an allusion to the wall of partition in the temple that kept Gentiles from intruding into areas reserved only for Jews. It effectively segregated the two peoples and let everyone know that the Jews were "better, more favored, more loved than the Gentiles." And for thousands of years, it would have been hard to argue that case based on human perception. And so everyone got very used to that idea, despite the many clues to the contrary that God Himself dropped all through the Old Testament.

That physical barrier, by the way, had a theological aspect to it. You see, it was more than just a wall in the Temple that kept the Jews and Gentiles separate; it was an entire body of commands that specifically did so. Mind you, there was a great need for the separation when Israel became a nation and all the years she lived at risk of being sucked into the Gentiles' idolatry. But the barrier that once served to keep Israel pure, along the way turned into a barrier that also kept the Gentiles dirty whether they wanted to be or not.

But on the rejoicing side, we find that *God hath broken down the middle wall of partition between us.* This wall that became so beloved by the Jews, this physical and theological barrier that allowed them special access to God but no one else, was broken down by a carpenter from Nazareth. And that phrase "broken down" is from the very first word any Greek student ever learns, the little word *luo*, meaning to break, demolish, and destroy.

Jesus did not tweak the wall; He did not renovate the wall; He did not even make a little opening in the wall; He obliterated the wall. So much so that Paul was able to say, "*he is our peace, who hath made both one.*" Those three little words "made both one" are earth-shattering. The idea that God would not just allow Jews and Gentiles to be together in the family, but would actually go so far as to make one unique body out of them was unfathomable to Jews, even to many Jewish believers!

But He did just that. And He did so on the basis of the fact that Christ is "our peace." In other words, we have the ability to come together like this because Jesus did not just *give* Jewish and Gentile believers peace with each other; He *is* the peace that we have with each other and with God. We both have Him as our Lord and Savior, He supersedes anything that came before or will come after, and therefore we are one in Him and have peace with each other.

He continues this thought in verse fifteen:

Ephesians 2:15 *Having abolished in his flesh the enmity, even the law of commandments contained in ordinances; for to make in himself of twain one new man, so making peace;*

The wording here is beautiful. This institutionalized reciprocal enmity between the Jews and Gentiles, Christ abolished it in His own flesh. Barnes said, "By the sacrifice of his body on the cross. It was not by instruction merely; it was not by communicating the knowledge of God; it was not as a teacher; it was not by the mere exertion of power; it was by his flesh--his human nature--and this can mean only that he did it by his sacrifice of himself." (Linder)

That is well said. Put another way, Jesus did not *teach* the enmity away; He *died* the enmity away.

This enmity was *"the law of commandments contained in ordinances."*

Barnes, once again, gives a very good take on this phrase, saying:

> "This does not refer to the moral law, which was not the cause of the alienation, and which was not abolished by the death of Christ, but to the laws commanding sacrifices, festivals, fasts, etc., which constituted the peculiarity of the Jewish system. These were the occasion of the enmity between the Jews and the Gentiles, and these were abolished by the great sacrifice which the Redeemer made; and of course when that was made, the purpose for which these laws were instituted was accomplished, and they ceased to be of value and to be binding." (Linder)

Paul dealt with that as well when writing to the Galatians:

Galatians 4:9 *But now, after that ye have known God, or rather are known of God, how turn ye again to the weak and beggarly elements, whereunto ye desire again to be in bondage?* **10** *Ye observe days, and months, and times, and years.*

These days, times, months, and years, all of the feasts and festivals and rituals that served to keep Jews and Gentiles apart were an enmity that Christ Himself did away with when He died on Calvary. And He did so *"for to make in himself of twain* [of two, of believing Jews and believing Gentiles] *one new man, so making peace."*

That "one new man" is the body of Christ, Christianity. Jews could never really be Gentiles, Gentiles could never really be Jews, but both Jews and Gentiles can really be Christians which was God's goal for all of humanity the entire time. It was His goal to have all men reconciled to their Creator through His Son, Jesus, and therefore, reconciled to one another as well.

If we are first and foremost anything (Jew, Gentile, American, Black, White) and secondly a "Christian," then we are not Christians at all! Our identity in Christ comes before any other identity, no exceptions. And that is the only basis upon which there can ever be peace in the hateful world of mankind!

The thought continues yet again into verse sixteen:

Ephesians 2:16 *And that he might reconcile both unto God in one body by the cross, having slain the enmity thereby:*

Mankind's main problem is not a skin problem; it is a sin problem. Jews and Gentiles and Americans and Russians and Saudi Arabians and Blacks and Whites and Reds and Browns are separated *from* God and need to be reconciled *to* God. And God made that possible *"in one body by the cross."* Simply put, what Jesus suffered on Calvary was enough judgment for our sins. And by "our" sins, here is what is meant:

1 John 2:2 *And he is the propitiation for our sins: and not for ours only, but also for the sins of the whole world.*

He did not die for the sins of Jews or Gentiles or black or white, and He certainly did not die for the sins of the "elect." He very specifically died for the sins of the whole world. And Ephesians 2:16 lets us know, ironically enough, that when Jesus died, He did some "killing" as well. Look at it again:

Ephesians 2:16 *And that he might reconcile both unto God in one body by the cross, having **slain** the enmity thereby:*

The enmity here in verse sixteen is a bit different from the enmity in verse fifteen. Verse fifteen dealt more with the enmity between Jew and Gentile; the enmity in verse sixteen is that between God and man. Both Jew and Gentile are alienated from God, and both Jew and Gentile have equal access to God through the sacrifice of Christ on Calvary.

Everywhere you look in these verses, you find the wreckage of old walls, and it really is a grand wreckage!

A gracious welcome

Ephesians 2:17 *And came and preached peace to you which were afar off, and to them that were nigh.*

You can easily tell by the way this sentence starts that the thought starts in the last sentence:

Ephesians 2:16 *And that he might reconcile both unto God in one body by the cross, having slain the enmity thereby:*

17 *And came and preached peace to you which were afar off, and to them that were nigh.*

Jesus reconciled both Jew and Gentile to God by what He did on Calvary; He ended the enmity between God and man, and He came and preached about that peace "*to you which were afar off* (Gentiles), *and to them that were nigh*" (Jews).

Far off. Nigh. Those things sound so very different! But they are no different at all when it gets right down to it; both "far off" and "near" are still not there! And that is why Jesus came and preached peace to both, not to one.

But from the Gentile's perspective, this was a truly glorious welcome. Those who are "far off" understand the treasure they are being offered far more easily than those who have lived next door to the treasure!

Ephesians 2:18 *For through him we both have access by one Spirit unto the Father.*

This verse, in just a handful of simple words, was like a punch to the gut for any Jew who fancied themselves better than any Gentile. But on the flip side, it was like the balm of Gilead to any Gentile who understood what was being offered them. Through Christ, we both equally, Jew or Gentile, have access by the Holy Spirit to God the Father. There is nothing on earth that even remotely compares. If we could stack all of the earthly promises made to the Jews on the left side and this one promise made to all on the right, the land and kingdom on the left would seem like plastic trinkets compared to the incomparable eternal treasure on the left.

We are not being offered a human high priest; we are being offered direct access to the throne of God.

We are not being offered land in the Middle East; we are being offered heaven.

We are not being offered a seventy-year lifespan to live as God's chosen human people; we are being offered eternity to live as His bride.

A glorious wonder

Ephesians 2:19 *Now therefore ye are no more strangers and foreigners, but fellowcitizens with the saints, and of the household of God;*

Therefore, because of what Christ did, the situation for the Gentiles has changed drastically. Adam Clarke explained it this way:

> "Formerly, when any of them came to Jerusalem, being *xenoi*, strangers, they had no kind of rights whatever; nor could they, as mere heathens, settle among them. Again, if any of them, convinced of the errors of the Gentiles, acknowledged the God of Israel, but did not receive circumcision, he might dwell in the land, but he had no right to the blessings of the covenant; such might be called *paroikoi*, sojourners-persons who have no property in the land, and may only rent a house for the time being."(6:441)

But now, as verse nineteen phrases it, believing Gentiles are "fellow citizens." Again, you would be hard-pressed to find a phrase that more forcefully describes how thoroughly God has brought believing Gentiles onto an equal plane with believing Jews. And yet, to somehow manage to make it even more powerful, he moves from terms of nationalism to terms of family, saying that believing Gentiles are of the *household* of God! Such a concept was almost beyond fathoming for any Jews of that day, a glorious wonder indeed.

And yet the wonder continued on into the next verse:

Ephesians 2:20 *And are built upon the foundation of the apostles and prophets, Jesus Christ himself being the chief corner stone;*

And, meaning "in addition to being fellowcitizens and of the household of God," we who believe are also *"built upon the foundation of the apostles and prophets, Jesus Christ himself being the chief corner stone."*

The Gentiles never had any God-sent apostles or prophets; all of those were to and from and for the Jews. But now, they find those very same prophets and apostles as their own personal foundation of faith – a foundation that has no less than Christ the Messiah as its chief cornerstone, the block against which all others are aligned and measured.

As Paul continues speaking of this glorious wonder, he will now use a rather picturesque description:

Ephesians 2:21 *In whom all the building fitly framed together groweth unto an holy temple in the Lord:*

Examining the subject and verb of this verse apart from all else will show you the picturesque description I am referring to:

"The building groweth."

Buildings do not "grow." People may add onto them, but they do not grow. But the building he is speaking of is not timber and tile; it is flesh and bone. We, believers in Christ, are that building. And when he says, "all the building," we know that he is yet again alluding to both Jewish and Gentile believers. We all, this building of flesh and bone that has believed on Christ, have been *"fitly framed together"* by God and are growing from a mere building into a temple. He is taking disparate parts that never did fit together in times past, and is not only making them fit perfectly together now, but is growing all of us together into a glorious structure of worship. But not just worship:

Ephesians 2:22 *In whom ye also are builded together for an habitation of God through the Spirit.*

God's purpose in saving any of us is for Him to come and live inside of us through the Holy Spirit before we ever get to go live with Him forever in heaven. The dwelling together is so pleasant to our Creator that He makes a way for us to do it now, Jews and Gentiles together in Him.

He has made rubble of the wall and produced riches out of that rubble.

Chapter Seven

The Messenger to the Messy

Ephesians 3:1 *For this cause I Paul, the prisoner of Jesus Christ for you Gentiles,* **2** *If ye have heard of the dispensation of the grace of God which is given me to you-ward:* **3** *How that by revelation he made known unto me the mystery; (as I wrote afore in few words,* **4** *Whereby, when ye read, ye may understand my knowledge in the mystery of Christ)* **5** *Which in other ages was not made known unto the sons of men, as it is now revealed unto his holy apostles and prophets by the Spirit;* **6** *That the Gentiles should be fellowheirs, and of the same body, and partakers of his promise in Christ by the gospel:* **7** *Whereof I was made a minister, according to the gift of the grace of God given unto me by the effectual working of his power.*

God tore down the middle wall of partition between the Jew and the Gentile and between Himself and man. The Gentiles were now admitted onto the "privileged side" of things. Paul, as the apostle to the Gentiles, was truly grateful for that. But he also knew full well that the people coming his way were not exactly the cream of humanity's crop.

He was, in so many words, the messenger to the messy.

A personal reminder

Ephesians 3:1 *For this cause I Paul, the prisoner of Jesus Christ for you Gentiles,*

There is absolutely nothing metaphorical about these words. Paul was very literally a prisoner because of his efforts to win the Gentiles to Christ. He was imprisoned at Philippi, he was imprisoned in Caesarea, he was imprisoned in Rome, and those are just the imprisonments that we know about! It is likely that he was behind bars even more times that we do not know about.

Just from what we do know, though, Paul spent roughly five and half years in custody before he was finally martyred. And all of it was because he was the apostle to the Gentiles.

But Paul did not take offense at this, and he certainly did not become bitter. In fact, in this verse, he calls himself *"the prisoner of Jesus Christ."* And that attitude explains why he took all of his imprisonments and suffering so joyfully.

If the bars keeping you in are Christ's bars instead of man's, you can be joyful about the bars.

When we look at the trials and tribulations that we encounter for being Christians as an honor given to us by God rather than as an insult given by man, it changes our entire perspective. Here is how Jesus Himself put it:

Matthew 5:11 *Blessed are ye, when men shall revile you, and persecute you, and shall say all manner of evil against you falsely, for my sake.* **12** *Rejoice, and be exceeding glad: for great is your reward in heaven: for so persecuted they the prophets which were before you.*

Paul really got this. He knew that his sufferings came because of him being the apostle to the Gentiles, but he also knew that those sufferings were an honor from the hand of Christ Himself. And he took the time in this verse to remind the converts in Ephesus of that very personal truth. This was a reminder that would serve to bring him and the people he loved closer together and make them much more willing to receive any difficult truth he had to confront them with.

A powerful revelation

Ephesians 3:2 *If ye have heard of the dispensation of the grace of God which is given me to you-ward:* **3** *How that by revelation he made known unto me the mystery; (as I wrote afore in few words,* **4** *Whereby, when ye read, ye may understand my knowledge in the mystery of Christ)* **5** *Which in other ages was not made known unto the sons of men, as it is now revealed unto* *his holy apostles and prophets by the Spirit;* **6** *That the Gentiles should be fellowheirs, and of the same body, and partakers of his promise in Christ by the gospel:*

As you can see, there is a parenthetical thought in these verses. Whenever you come across one of those in Scripture, take a moment and read the passage without it so you can understand what the main thought is and separate it from the accompanying thought.

Here, then, was the main thought:

If ye have heard of the dispensation of the grace of God which is given me to you-ward: **3** *How that by revelation he made known unto me the mystery;...* **5** *Which in other ages was not made known unto the sons of men, as it is now revealed unto his holy apostles and prophets by the Spirit;* **6** *That the Gentiles should be fellowheirs, and of the same body, and partakers of his promise in Christ by the gospel:*

And here, then, was the accompanying thought:

(as I wrote afore in few words, Whereby, when ye read, ye may understand my knowledge in the mystery of Christ)

Let's deal with the accompanying thought first. Paul was reminding them that he had already briefly written to them about this subject matter, the fact that God would bring the Gentiles into the household of salvation on equal plane with believing Jews. The question that arises from this, though, is what writing he is referring to. The position that the majority of commentators have taken through the years is that he is talking about what he has already mentioned to them in the previous chapter. And that would certainly fit because the subject matter he is referring to here is exactly what he wrote about in chapter two.

Others believe that there was a previous letter that he wrote to the church at Ephesus and that he was referring to that previous letter.

But since there is no evidence of a previous letter, and since we do clearly know that the previous chapter spoke of this very topic, the safest thing for us to assume is that he was referring to what he wrote in that previous chapter.

Look at the last portion of the parenthetical thought again:

Whereby, when ye read, ye may understand my knowledge in the mystery of Christ.

In other words, Paul was encouraging them to refer back to what he had already written on the subject so that they would understand his knowledge in this mystery that Christ had made known to him.

Now let us deal with the main thought in these verses.

Ephesians 3:2 *If ye have heard of the dispensation of the grace of God which is given me to you-ward:*

This is the second time Paul has used the word dispensation in the book of Ephesians. As a reminder, here was the first one:

Ephesians 1:10 *That in the dispensation of the fulness of times he might gather together in one all things in Christ, both which are in heaven, and which are on earth; even in him:*

When we studied this verse, I told you that the word dispensation is only used four times in Scripture, all in the writings of Paul. I also told you that in all four usages of this word it comes from the word *oikonomia*, and we get our word *economy* from it. It means "management, administration, and stewardship." Adam Clarke defines it this way, "a plan for the management of any sort of business." (6:433)

With that reminder, look again at verse two:

Ephesians 3:2 *If ye have heard of the dispensation* [the stewardship] *of the grace of God which is given me to you-ward:*

God put Paul as the steward, the manager, if you will, of making sure the Gentile world heard the gospel of the grace of God. He entrusted this former hater of the Gentiles to this labor of love for the messy Gentiles.

Now look at the rest of the main thought once again:

3 *How that by revelation he made known unto me the mystery;...* **5** *Which in other ages was not made known unto the sons of men, as it is now revealed unto his holy apostles and prophets by the Spirit;* **6** *That the Gentiles should be fellowheirs, and of the same body, and partakers of his promise in Christ by the gospel:*

By revelation, by God through the Holy Spirit personally breathing out this information to Paul and to other holy apostles and prophets, Paul came to understand what Old Testament prophets did not understand, that the Gentiles, messiness and all, should be fellow heirs and of the same body and partakers of his promise in Christ by the gospel.

This was a powerful revelation. In fact, it is the revelation that changed the entire messy world. Let me read you part of a column that explains some of those changes.

"Former professor of sociology Dr. Alvin Schmidt notes Elwood Cubberly's observation that the biblical teachings of Jesus Christ challenged 'almost everything for which the Roman world had stood' (How Christianity Changed the World, Schmidt, p. 44). Dr. James Kennedy writes, 'Life was expendable prior to Christianity's influence… In those days abortion was rampant. Abandonment was commonplace: it was common for infirmed babies or unwanted little ones to be taken out into the forest or the mountainside, to be consumed by wild animals or to starve… They often abandoned female babies because women were considered inferior" (What If Jesus Had Never Been Born?, pp. 9–11).

"The Romans promoted brutal gladiatorial contests where thousands of slaves, condemned criminals and prisoners of war mauled and slaughtered each other for the amusement of cheering audiences. Roman authors indicate that 'sexual activity between men and women had become highly promiscuous and essentially depraved before and during the time that Christians appeared in Roman society' and that homosexuality was widespread among pagan Greeks and Romans, especially men with boys (Schmidt, pp. 79–86). Women were relegated to a low status in society, where they received little schooling, could not speak in public and were viewed as the property of their husbands (Schmidt, pp. 97–102).

"As professing Christianity spread in the region, those parts of its teachings that corresponded to biblical truths had a profound impact. Pagan practices were confronted with biblical principles concerning the status of women and the importance of the family (Ephesians

5:22–33; 6:1–4), the sanctity of human life as made in God's image (Genesis 1:26), and the sinfulness of sexual immorality and homosexuality (1 Corinthians 6:9–10). Eventually, Roman emperors even outlawed the branding of criminals and crucifixion and terminated the brutal gladiatorial contests that had flourished for nearly seven centuries—implementing one of the most important reforms in the moral history of mankind (Schmidt, p. 63–65). In the words of historian Christopher Dawson, the changes brought about by the spread of these ideas marked 'the beginning of a new era in world history.' (Religion and the Rise of Western Culture, p. 25).

"Such changes were not limited to the West. The influence of biblical principles abolished suttee in India—the practice of burning widows on the funeral pyre of their husband. It stopped the killing of wives and concubines when tribal chiefs died in Africa, discouraged cannibalism, and helped to end the global slave trade in the 1800s" (Kennedy, pp. 16–17). (Winnail)

If I may give you a short and simple summary of that, the gospel of Jesus Christ being brought to the Gentiles gave us the civilized world that mankind has more or less enjoyed for 2,000 years now. The fact that our civilized world is now decaying and descending into absolute anarchy and savagery is a direct result of the fact that the gospel message is now being rejected wholesale by the world, both Jew and Gentile.

A precious responsibility

Ephesians 3:7 *Whereof I was made a minister, according to the gift of the grace of God given unto me by the effectual working of his power.*

The word "whereof" that begins this verse refers back to the gospel in the previous verse. Paul was made a minister of the gospel. Interestingly, when we use the word minister, we normally think of a preacher, and Paul certainly was a preacher, but this word for minister is from the word *diakonos*, and we get our English word deacon from it. But in this case, it is not referring to the *office* of a deacon but to the *attitude* of a deacon. You see, that word means "servant." Paul did not view himself as a celebrity as so many preachers today do. He did not believe that people should wait on him hand and foot. He did not think that he was to be placed on a pedestal and others were to be regarded as beneath him. He viewed the gospel ministry as a service and himself as a servant.

That is, by the way, the exact right way to view the ministry. It is also the exact attitude that Christ Himself took:

Mark 10:45 *For even the Son of man came not to be ministered unto, but to minister, and to give his life a ransom for many.*

Any preacher that goes into the ministry with the idea of enriching himself or empowering himself is a devil that should never be allowed behind any pulpit anywhere.

Look at where Paul said his call to ministry originated from:

...according to the gift of the grace of God given unto me by the effectual working of his power.

He correctly viewed it as a gift and as the grace of God at work in his life through the effectual working, the *energia,* of God's power.

Paul remembered his past wickedness. He even recognized his present weakness. He spoke of both of those things at length throughout his writings. Paul understood better than most that being allowed into the ministry is a precious responsibility and is always to be treated as such. And if any of us are going to be the messengers to the messy in these wicked days, days in which everyone is carrying cell phones and recording things, days in which every word that we say is going to make its way online and be repeated over and over again, we better take this precious responsibility seriously.

And we better make sure that there is nothing in the messenger that undermines the message.

Chapter Eight
The Fellowship of the Mystery

Ephesians 3:8 *Unto me, who am less than the least of all saints, is this grace given, that I should preach among the Gentiles the unsearchable riches of Christ;* **9** *And to make all men see what is the fellowship of the mystery, which from the beginning of the world hath been hid in God, who created all things by Jesus Christ:* **10** *To the intent that now unto the principalities and powers in heavenly places might be known by the church the manifold wisdom of God,* **11** *According to the eternal purpose which he purposed in Christ Jesus our Lord:* **12** *In whom we have boldness and access with confidence by the faith of him.*

Some years ago, my son Caleb and I got to go to a rather unique place, at least for us. We got to go to a swanky dinner at the country club. Neither of us had ever been to a place like that before. The meal was delicious, although, to be quite honest, I could not identify some of the things that I was eating. Everything was served on fine China. And most of the people in the room were multimillionaires.

And then there was Caleb and me, multihundredaires...

The reason we were allowed in there with all of those incredibly wealthy people is because a few years earlier, a startup bank in our area had put out a notice asking for investors, and I invested the whopping sum of $550 into it. They were really desperate for investors!

Anyway, because I invested in the bank, when they had an important meeting about the bank's future, I was invited to this swanky affair at the country club. I got to fellowship with people way more powerful and wealthy than myself – and I even looked around to make sure I used the right silverware at the right time. Nonetheless, I definitely felt like the odd, uncouth Gentile at the table!

In our text, Paul had just finished talking about the fact that he was the messenger to the messy. He, a devout Jew, a former despiser of the Gentiles, had been appointed by God as the apostle to the Gentiles. Paul would spend the rest of his life being persecuted and tormented and eventually martyred because of his passion to fulfill that calling and take the gospel to the Gentile world.

It was not just perplexing to the Jews who saw him do that; it was an absolute mystery, as was God's entire purpose for all of it. And they became Paul's bitter, sworn enemies because of it all. But that mystery did not just come with foes; it also came with a wonderful fellowship.

A humble truth

Ephesians 3:8 *Unto me, who am less than the least of all saints, is this grace given, that I should preach among the Gentiles the unsearchable riches of Christ;*

When Paul wrote his first epistle to the church at Corinth, he called himself by a very humble and self-abasing title:

1 Corinthians 15:9 *For I am the least of the apostles, that am not meet to be called an apostle, because I persecuted the church of God.*

That was some pretty impressive humility on his part; truthfully, based on impact, most of us would regard him as the greatest of the apostles. But he did not. He genuinely regarded himself as the least, meaning the smallest and the least important of the apostles. The least of the apostles, though, would still be very rarefied air, still incredibly elite company. There were only a handful of apostles in all of Scripture and in all of history. It was a one-generation office that very few ever held.

But as Paul put pen to parchment and wrote the epistle to the church at Ephesus, we find him using a term far more humble still:

Ephesians 3:8 *Unto me, <u>who am less than the least of all saints</u>, is this grace given, that I should preach among the Gentiles the unsearchable riches of Christ;*

To the Corinthians, he called himself the least of the apostles. To the Ephesians, he called himself less than the least of all saints. The saints, *tone hagione*, simply means "the ones who have been made holy, the saved." It is a way to refer to every Christian and all Christians. Just in the days in which Paul wrote this letter, Christians were already numbering in the hundreds of thousands. And Paul called himself less than the least of all of them.

This kind of consistent humility on Paul's part is most certainly one of the main reasons that he was so effective in his ministry to the Gentiles. You can search through Scripture and history at length, and you will find very few examples of Jews being humble to the Gentiles. They almost universally believed themselves to be far better and far more worthy than the Gentiles, and they openly despised and looked down on the Gentiles.

Yet one day, this prominent Jew, Saul of Tarsus, came by preaching the gospel. And he preached it as a man who realized that he himself was not worthy of it. He went on in verse eight to say that it was pure grace given to him, that he should be allowed to preach among the Gentiles the unsearchable riches of Christ. He often worked with his hands to meet his own needs rather than be seen as someone who was just in it for money. He rebuked his own kind, Peter and others, when they behaved arrogantly to the Gentiles.

To Paul, it was always all about Christ. He used the words *the unsearchable riches of Christ* at the end of the verse to describe what he was preaching, indicating that no matter how long we study or how deep we delve into it, we will never exhaust the riches of the person of Christ or the salvation that He offers.

There is nothing alluring about a Christian witness who comes in pride and arrogance. There is nothing about a haughty believer that makes sinners want to come and lay down their lives at the feet of Christ. Paul was the most successful soul winner likely in human history, and the humility he showed was largely responsible for it.

A hidden treasure

Ephesians 3:9 *And to make all men see what is the fellowship of the mystery, which from the beginning of the world hath been hid in God, who created all things by Jesus Christ:* **10** *To the intent that now unto the principalities and powers in heavenly places might be known by the church the manifold wisdom of God,*

From the way verse nine begins, you may quickly be aware that it is a continuation of a sentence that began earlier. In fact, like so many of these very long sentences that we have observed thus far in the book of Ephesians, this one started in verse eight and will not end until verse twelve. So look at verse eight along with the first part of verse nine in order to help understand what Paul was saying:

Ephesians 3:8 *Unto me, who am less than the least of all saints, is this grace given, that I should preach among the Gentiles the unsearchable riches of Christ;* **9a** *And to make all men see what is the fellowship of the mystery...*

Verse eight and the first part of verse nine describe the two-part mission that God gave to Paul. Paul was to preach among the Gentiles the unsearchable riches of Christ and to make all men see the fellowship of this mystery of God. So, what is he talking about when he uses the phrase "the fellowship of the mystery?" He sounds very much like he is going on a quest with elves and dwarves and wizards and may never come back alive!

But Paul did not have anything so Tolkienesque in mind. He actually had something far more dramatic and consequential. Mind you, the picture of unlike things (dwarves, elves, men, etc.) coming together as one body does very much fit what Paul had in mind about the word fellowship. It is from the word *koinonia*, and it infers a very tight-knit association, a group that has come together in unity. But this fellowship was not the fellowship of the ring but the fellowship of the mystery. It did not have to do with getting to the fires of Mount Doom but with escaping the fires of hell. And it was not a fellowship that would disband once a particular quest was done; it was a fellowship that would joyfully be bound together for all eternity.

The mystery Paul mentions here has already been spoken of three times by this point in the book of Ephesians:

Ephesians 1:9 *Having made known unto us the **mystery** of his will, according to his good pleasure which he hath purposed in himself:*

Ephesians 3:3 *How that by revelation he made known unto me the **mystery**; (as I wrote afore in few words,*

Ephesians 3:4 *Whereby, when ye read, ye may understand my knowledge in the **mystery** of Christ)*

It will go on to be mentioned twice more, in Ephesians 5:32 and Ephesians 6:13. No other book of the Bible even comes close in the amount of mentions of this mystery because no other book deals so specifically with the mystery, namely that Jews and Gentiles would be brought together on an equal plane in God's household of faith. Again, the book of Ephesians is all about the fact that from before the very beginning, before there ever even was time or space, God predestined to save not just believing Jews but believing Gentiles as well, and He predestined that those Gentiles would not just be allowed in the Beloved, but accepted, adored in the Beloved. And how many people did God intend to get Paul to see that mystery?

All men.

God is really big on having everyone see and understand the gospel message. And the word He used for "see" is a pretty interesting word, the word *photisai*. You may hear our English word *photo* in that. And that is because photographs are reproductions of what the light transmits to our eyes. This word means "to give light, to illuminate," or, as we often put it, to turn the lights on. God turns the lights on for everyone at some point. No one will ever die and go to hell for lack of light; they will only die and go to hell out of unwillingness to accept what God shows them.

Now look at verse nine again, and this time let's focus on the last half of it.

Ephesians 3:9 *And to make all men see what is the fellowship of the mystery,* <u>*which from the beginning of the world hath been hid in God, who created all things by Jesus Christ:*</u>

This plan of God to bring the Gentiles into the household of faith seemed very new, out of left field, to the Jews. And that is one reason why they reacted so vehemently against it. But the fact that it seemed new to them did not make it wrong. You see, God does not owe us all information upfront. Truthfully, He does not owe us any information ever. The fact that He ever tells us anything is just pure graciousness on His part.

So this plan of God to include the Gentiles in salvation was always "the plan." But God, in His sovereignty, chose to hide that plan in Himself from the beginning of time and had every right to do so. When it comes to God's dealings with man, it is not the length of time something has been known that makes it good or bad; it is the source from whence it comes. The fact that this plan was hidden in God all this time and then revealed by God should have been enough for everyone to be on board with it immediately.

But this is the exact same conundrum we often face in our own lives with our own stubborn wills. God shows us part of the plan, and we foolishly assume that He has shown us everything and that nothing will ever change. And yet He has every right at any point to give us, as Paul Harvey would put it, "the rest of the story."

Having the Gentiles as equally accepted and adored as the Jews was definitely a very dramatic "rest of the story."

Now, with something that drastic, there would need to be a recognized authority behind it, a justification of so doing, if you will, in order for people to be willing to get behind it. And God gave us that justification at the end of the verse in the words <u>*who created all things by Jesus Christ.*</u>

We find here another statement of many in Scripture that Jesus Christ, the second member of the Trinity, was the One to whom God entrusted the creation of all things. You and I have a universe to live in specifically because Jesus Christ made it. But in the context of the discussion at hand, we find the justification I spoke of a moment ago for this radical change from the Old Testament economy to the New Testament economy. The fact that God created all things through Christ is more than enough justification for everyone to be willing to say, "Yes sir!" when God speaks on any subject. How can we, the created, take umbrage with the decisions God makes with His creation, especially when those decisions are good and gracious decisions toward humanity?

Ephesians 3:10 *To the intent that now unto the principalities and powers in heavenly places might be known by the church the manifold wisdom of God,*

"To the intent" means "in order that." It is a statement of intention, as is obvious from the very word intent; it lets us know some of what God had in mind by what He was doing in all of this. His intent, in this case, was to demonstrate to the entire universe, from the church all the way up to the very principalities and powers in heavenly places the manifold wisdom of God.

Let me put it this way. Nobody has to know anything for God to be magnificent. But God, in His magnificence, desires us to know. This mystery of God may have been secret from the beginning, but it was never intended to remain a secret. For us, the recipients, the church, that is a very good thing. We get saved by the knowledge of the plan of God. For these principalities and powers in heavenly places, which is speaking of angelic beings of different ranks and orders, they get excited by the knowledge of the plan of God. In fact, look at a phrase used elsewhere about this same topic:

1 Peter 1:12 *Unto whom it was revealed, that not unto themselves, but unto us they did minister the things, which are now reported unto you by them that have preached the gospel unto you with the Holy Ghost sent down from heaven;* <u>*which things the angels desire to look into*</u>.

The word for desire here is *epithumousin,* and it is such a strong word for desire that it is sometimes translated as lust. The angels are hungry to learn about redemption. None of the fallen angels were ever offered a chance at it; none of the unfallen ever needed it; so all of them, for good or bad, are fascinated by it. And part of God's plan is to show them this hidden treasure.

A heavenly turn

Ephesians 3:11 *According to the eternal purpose which he purposed in Christ Jesus our Lord: 12 In whom we have boldness and access with confidence by the faith of him.*

All of this was *"According to the eternal purpose which he purposed in Christ Jesus our Lord."* And yet, it was at once both eternal and brand-new! Eternal to God? Yes. Brand new to the understanding of man? Yes, as well. Something we should be timid about? No, definitely not. Paul, speaking of Jesus, said we have both boldness and, not just access, but access with confidence by the faith of Him, Jesus. In other words, we have access to God the Father Himself through Jesus the Son. And we do not have to slink to the throne as if we do not belong there; we can come just as comfortably and confidently as Christ Himself.

In this, when Paul uses the word "we," we deal with a bit of a different situation than just the Gentiles being allowed access on an equal plane with Jewish believers. You see, though Jews knew they were the people of God, and the Gentiles were just now finding out that they could be the people of God, neither Jew nor Gentile could formerly come before God the Father, and certainly not with boldness! The high priest could only go to the holy of holies one time a year before the representative presence of God and only while carrying blood for his sins and the sin of the people.

But through Christ, any believer, Jew or Gentile, can bow the heart in prayer and have direct access to the very throne room of God anytime, day or night. And this marks the greatest heavenly turn there has ever been. Whereas formerly the message being sent was "God is too holy, and you are too sinful, don't even think about coming into my presence," now, through Christ, the message is "You are just as holy as my Son, and you are welcome in my presence at any time." And the people first seeing those words in print were mostly Gentiles. God took the least likely candidates to ever be in His presence and welcomed them in, welcomed *us* in, making them/us part of the fellowship.

Unlike my Country Club experience, it was not my investment in the matter that gained me access, nor will it be your investment in the matter that gains you access. The price is far too high for all of us! The only thing that will ever serve as an acceptable price for access is the sacrifice that Christ made on our behalf on Calvary. And when we lay aside our pride and willingly receive what Christ has offered us, we truly become part of *The Fellowship of the Mystery*.

Chapter Nine

It's Worth It All

Ephesians 3:13 *Wherefore I desire that ye faint not at my tribulations for you, which is your glory.* **14** *For this cause I bow my knees unto the Father of our Lord Jesus Christ,* **15** *Of whom the whole family in heaven and earth is named,* **16** *That he would grant you, according to the riches of his glory, to be strengthened with might by his Spirit in the inner man;* **17** *That Christ may dwell in your hearts by faith; that ye, being rooted and grounded in love,* **18** *May be able to comprehend with all saints what is the breadth, and length, and depth, and height;* **19** *And to know the love of Christ, which passeth knowledge, that ye might be filled with all the fulness of God.* **20** *Now unto him that is able to do exceeding abundantly above all that we ask or think, according to the power that worketh in us,* **21** *Unto him be glory in the church by Christ Jesus throughout all ages, world without end. Amen.*

Paul just got done telling the church in Ephesus about the fellowship of the mystery and that because of it, they had boldness and not just access to the Father, but access with confidence. But he will now bring things down to more practical and painful matters. And yet, the brightness in his heart will not dim even a little; Paul knew that it was worth it all.

A purpose for trials

Ephesians 3:13 *Wherefore I desire that ye faint not at my tribulations for you, which is your glory.*

The word wherefore takes us back to what came before it, namely the glory of the fellowship of the mystery in Christ. Wherefore, because of that, Paul's desire was for Ephesians not to faint at the tribulations and trials he was undergoing on their behalf. He was very literally in prison at that moment, suffering because of taking the gospel to the Gentile world, including them. The purpose for his trials was his insistence on telling everyone about Christ. And yet, even in those trials for others, his fear and concern were not for himself but for them.

In short, he was worried that when the Ephesians learned of the hardships he was undergoing for them, they would do something horrible; he was worried that they would faint. And this word for faint, as you might suspect, has nothing to do with passing out. It is from the word *ekkakein*, and it means "to be spiritless, to be exhausted, to give in to evil, and to become a coward." It presents the picture of a person who has started off as a brave soldier for Christ, and then when the battle gets hot, waves the white flag of surrender and even goes so far as to join the other side.

That is the very last thing Paul wanted for the Ephesians, for anyone, really. And the last phrase of the verse, *which is your glory*, refers back to their not fainting. It is never a glory to faint in the face of a spiritual enemy or any adversity, and it is always a glory not to faint in the face of a spiritual enemy or any adversity. No one gives medals for "The Best Giver-Upper"; they give medals for valor.

Ephesians 3:14 *For this cause I bow my knees unto the Father of our Lord Jesus Christ,* **15** *Of whom the whole family in heaven and earth is named,* **16** *That he would grant you, according to the riches of his glory, to be strengthened with might by his Spirit in the inner man;*

Paul's opening phrase here means, "For this cause, because it is your glory not to faint, I bow my knees unto the Father of our Lord Jesus Christ." So Paul did not just want them not to faint, and he did not just instruct them not to faint; he went to prayer so that they would not faint. As to verse fifteen, Adam Clarke gives a good description of its meaning, saying:

"Believers in the Lord Jesus Christ on earth, the spirits of just men made perfect in a separate state, and all the holy angels in heaven, make but one family, of which God is the Father and Head. St. Paul does not say, of whom the families, as if each order formed a distinct household; but he says family, because they are all one, and of one. And all this family is named-derives its origin and being, from God, as children derive their name from him who is the father of the family." (6:446)

Paul's purpose in stating all of this, though, deals less with genealogical theology and more with his desire for them not to faint; these words are a "because," not a random fact. Because all of us who believe are the family of God along with all of the saints who have ever lived and all the angels in glory, we have a responsibility to our wonderful family and our great Father to stand strong. We are not just anybody; we are children of the King.

But if this standing strong in the face of adversity is solely a matter of our will and capabilities, we are obviously in a great deal of trouble. None of us are any match for the devil! Fortunately, as verse sixteen makes clear, we have a greater source than merely the willpower within us:

Ephesians 3:16 *That he would grant you, according to the riches of his glory, to be strengthened with might by his Spirit in the inner man;*

There is no Nautilus machine or set of free weights that will allow us to bench press or curl our spirit into a state of strength. If we are going to be strengthened in our inner man, it will need to come from God. And Paul was praying for that very thing on their behalf. We as well ought to pray for that very thing on our own behalf and on behalf of others. And this is not a trivial or secondary matter; this strength comes from "the riches of his glory" and is a product of the Holy Spirit Himself, the third member of the Trinity.

That is incomparably valuable strength both in derivation and delivery! And it is also the first of four very important "thats" that Paul had in mind for the Ephesians and us.

A powerful hope

Ephesians 3:17a *That Christ may dwell in your hearts by faith...*

This will be the second of four "thats" that Paul was praying for for his beloved Ephesian believers. Remember that the first one, in verse sixteen, was **that** they might be strengthened; the third one will be *"that ye, being rooted and grounded in love, May be able to comprehend with all saints what is the breadth, and length, and depth, and height; And to know the love of Christ, which passeth knowledge,"* and the fourth one will spring off of that one, as we will see at the end of verse nineteen and will be **that** they might be filled with the fulness of God.

This one, in verse seventeen, is *"**That** Christ may dwell in your hearts by faith."*

The believers in Ephesus were obviously saved; salvation, therefore, is not what Paul had in mind by this statement. The word dwell in this verse is from the word *katoikaysai*, and it means "to settle into." It is the difference between purchasing a house versus coming inside to live, making it your own, and turning it into a home. Christ paid the purchase price for us on Calvary, and when we receive Him as our Savior, His purchase of us becomes in force and complete. But that is far different from us allowing Him to settle in and make our bodies and our hearts His comfortable home. Saved people are often guilty of being carried to heaven by salvation while carrying the world in their hearts by carnality.

Yet this same faith that saves us and makes us His is able to sanctify us and make us comfortable to Him, a dwelling place of flesh and bones in which He feels at home. And that truly is the beginning of a powerful hope for us, a matter of life that will make us live like we are on the way to heaven rather than have us on the way to heaven while living like the world around us.

Now let's look at the third important "that."

Ephesians 3:17b... *that ye, being rooted and grounded in love,* **18** *May be able to comprehend with all saints what is the breadth, and length, and depth, and height;* **19** *And to know the love of Christ, which passeth knowledge...*

This "that" phrase in verse seventeen gives us both an agricultural and an architectural illustration for the truth it portrays. Rooted is an agricultural term and one that is very easy to understand. It is simply the picture of a plant or tree sending roots very deep into the ground for stability. Grounded is an architectural term meaning to lay a foundation. That also is easy to understand; the foundation is the base of the strength of an entire structure, without which it could not stand.

What does being rooted and grounded in love have to do with believers withstanding their trials? Verses eighteen and nineteen will give us the answer to that.

Ephesians 3:18 *May be able to comprehend with all saints what is the breadth, and length, and depth, and height;* **19** *And to know the love of Christ, which passeth knowledge, that ye might be filled with all the fulness of God.*

If we are truly rooted and grounded in love, not emotion, not a desire for advancement, not merely a fire escape from the wrath to come, if our salvation and our stand are rooted in love, we will not faint. And the reason we will not faint is because we will comprehend, we will understand, along with all saints, coming behind none of them in this important matter, the breadth, and length, and depth, and height of the love of Christ. The height is how high it goes, the depth is how low it goes, the length is how far it goes, and the breadth is to what extent it goes.

Some believers may not be able to understand eschatology as well as other believers. Some believers may not be able to understand ecclesiology as well as other believers. But all believers have the capacity to understand the love of Christ to the same degree as all other believers, all other saints. A Bible college professor can grasp the love of Christ thoroughly enough to withstand persecution and trials and temptations, and so can an old coal miner from West Virginia with a third-grade education.

And yet, in a divine paradox, the very next phrase we read about the love of God here is *"which passeth knowledge."* So how can we *"**know** the love of Christ, which passeth **knowledge**"*? How do we unravel that paradox? The answer is the difference between the natural that Paul feared for them and the supernatural that he desired for them. In their natural, fainting flesh, they had no capacity to truly know the love of Christ, nor do we. But through the revelation given to us by the Holy Spirit Himself, we can know the unknowable. This is revelation and illumination at work in our hearts.

And that brings us to the last of the four "thats": *that ye might be filled with all the fulness of God.*

This one, as I mentioned earlier, springs from the previous one. It is when we "know the love of Christ, which passeth knowledge" that we can be "filled with all the fulness of God." And, whether you yet realize it or not, that is a staggering statement that has just been made. And it should sound to you like something you have seen elsewhere in Scripture:

Colossians 2:9 *For in him* [in Christ] *dwelleth all the fulness of the Godhead bodily.*

These verses are saying very much the same thing. When Christ was in flesh on the earth, He behaved radically different than everyone around Him simply because, rather than being filled with a fleshly nature, He was filled completely with the nature of the Godhead, the Trinity. When we truly know the love of God, we can be likewise *"filled with all the fulness of God."* Our old nature can be as if it is not even there, and all of our behavior can spring out of the nature of God in us.

Mind you, unlike Christ, this will have to be a day-by-day choice and exercise on our behalf. He never had to choose it; it was and is consistently part of His nature. But we can choose it; we have that option. We have the option to be so fixated on the love of God and to be so filled with the love of God that our wicked, fleshly nature has no power in our lives, and all that springs forth is that which comes from the nature of Christ in us.

All of that really is a powerful hope.

A praise to God

Ephesians 3:20 *Now unto him that is able to do exceeding abundantly above all that we ask or think, according to the power that worketh in us,* **21** *Unto him be glory in the church by Christ Jesus throughout all ages, world without end. Amen.*

If these verses sound somewhat out of place, almost as if they belong at the end of the book, it is because, while they do not mark the end of the book, they do mark the end of the first act of the book, as it were. The first three and last three chapters of the book of Ephesians look and sound very different because they are very different. The first half of the book is very much about the divine, God's work on our behalf. The second half of the book will be very much about the daily, our work on God's behalf. The first half of the book is very much "God did this;" the second half is very much "now you do this."

And so Paul ends this first of two acts with a glorious spurt of praise for all that God has done.

He begins by reminding us that God *is able to do exceeding abundantly above all that we ask or think, according to the power that worketh in us*. And he has not changed subjects in this. The seemingly impossible work that he just described, us being filled with all the fullness of God, is possible after all because God is able to do exceedingly abundantly above all that we ask or think, according to the power that worketh in us. So, while we could never will ourselves to behave like God, God can work His power in us so that we do behave like God. And Paul's concluding praise to God for that is, "*Unto him be glory in the church by Christ Jesus throughout all ages, world without end. Amen.*"

How long will we be glorifying God for His work in us? We obviously start right now since it is "in the church by Christ Jesus." But it does not stop with the right now; it goes "throughout all ages, world without end." This tells us that it goes through every succeeding generation of mankind and then continues right on into eternity itself without any stopping point. Paul knew that we would be glorifying God forever and ever and ever and ever for His work in our lives. So, his trials were indeed worth it all. And the most logical thing he could think to say about something so marvelous was, "Amen, so be it."

Amen indeed.

Chapter Ten
A Worthy Walk

Ephesians 4:1 *I therefore, the prisoner of the Lord, beseech you that ye walk worthy of the vocation wherewith ye are called,* **2** *With all lowliness and meekness, with longsuffering, forbearing one another in love;* **3** *Endeavouring to keep the unity of the Spirit in the bond of peace.* **4** *There is one body, and one Spirit, even as ye are called in one hope of your calling;* **5** *One Lord, one faith, one baptism,* **6** *One God and Father of all, who is above all, and through all, and in you all.*

Having laid the spiritual foundation in the first half of his letter to the Ephesians, Paul will now spell out the practical outgrowth that is to follow from that foundation. Simply put, since God has been so very gracious to allow us into the household of faith, since He has, in fact, predestined us Gentiles to this high honor from eternity past, we surely ought to gladly live for Him here and now.

And He will begin to explain that with a bit of a talk about our walk.

An understanding that beckons us

Ephesians 4:1 *I therefore, the prisoner of the Lord, beseech you that ye walk worthy of the vocation wherewith ye are called,* **2** *With all lowliness and meekness, with longsuffering, forbearing one another in love;* **3** *Endeavouring to keep the unity of the Spirit in the bond of peace.*

As with so much of the Epistle to the Ephesians, these three verses make up one long sentence. Paul starts, though, in the very same place that he began in chapter three. Look at the beginnings of these two chapters back-to-back:

Ephesians 3:1 *For this cause I Paul, the prisoner of Jesus Christ...*

Ephesians 4:1 *I therefore, the prisoner of the Lord...*

Once again, Paul was reminding the Ephesian believers of the high price he was paying in order to have brought them the gospel. An emotional appeal? Absolutely. A justifiable appeal? Absolutely as well.

So what is it that Paul wanted from them, or rather, for them? Was it some outlandish, unreasonable thing? Certainly not:

Ephesians 4:1 *I therefore, the prisoner of the Lord, beseech you that ye walk worthy of the vocation wherewith ye are called,*

Let's define a few words as we begin to unfold the truth of this verse. Worthy is from the word *axios,* and it means "suitably, in a manner worthy of." So, he was asking them to walk suitably based on some particular thing. And the particular thing he had in mind was *"the vocation wherewith ye are called."* When we see the word vocation, we normally think of a job that we hold. But in this case, it is from the word *klaysis,* and it means "a calling, an invitation," and sometimes "an invitation to a feast." So what Paul has in mind is not the task of being a Christian, but the fact that we have been invited to such a high station to begin with! In other words, he was driving at something like this:

> "Look, you were lost, pagan heathens with a horrible background. Spiritually, you were eating out of life's landfill. But Christ specifically sent me by your way to invite you into the palace of salvation. There is no garbage to root through; you will be provided with the very best that heaven has to offer.
>
> "But since that is the case, you need to act differently. Wearing filthy rags and burping out loud and talking with food in your mouth will never be appropriate in such a divine setting. Clean up, use your best manners, and act like you belong because you do."

We who are saved need to act saved, not lost. We do not need to act like children of the devil; we need to act like children of the King. In modern vernacular, we need to up our game! And the next couple of verses will tell us several things that Paul had in mind when He wrote these instructions.

Ephesians 4:2 *With all lowliness and meekness, with longsuffering, forbearing one another in love;* **3** *Endeavouring to keep the unity of the Spirit in the bond of peace.*

The first part he covers in having us walk worthy of the vocation we have been called to is that we walk in lowliness and meekness. Lowliness is from the word *tapeinophrosunay*. It means "humility of mind, not being haughty or proud." Meekness is from the word *praotays,* and it means "gentleness and mildness." To package all of that in a simple form, these terms mean that we are not to be arrogant or needlessly caustic or condescending.

Now, please understand the balance in this. Paul will go on to couch our Christian walk in military terms in chapter six, picturing us as soldiers. He will use the words "*Stand, therefore,*" and "*having done all, to stand.*" So, Paul was not in the least commanding that we be doormats, and he certainly was not telling us to simply smile and nod as evil engulfs our families, churches, and land. But he was absolutely forbidding in us the arrogant, injurious, self-aggrandizing attitude that even many preachers seem far too often to develop.

I have heard fairly new Christians describe a preacher or two as jerks, and I was not able to honestly disagree. And many Christians in the pew are just as bad. Yes, we are to stand for the truth without wavering. But all the while, we are to be lowly and meek, not Christian shock-jocks.

The second part he covers in having us walk worthy of the vocation we have been called to is that we are to be "*forbearing one another in love."* That word forebearing is from the word *aneckomai*, and it means "to hold up, to sustain, to endure." When used in the phrase "*forbearing one another in love,"* we (perhaps unhappily!) learn that we are to be, in so many words, "putting up with each other!" And if you have been around Christians for any length of time at all, you know that can often be a really difficult thing.

Ironically, Paul, who wrote these words, at one point found that he was unwilling to put up with John Mark and unable to put up with Barnabas. This does not make the message untrue, but it does tell us how much effort it often takes!

When we get to heaven, none of us will have to "put up with" any of us because all of us will be on the same page about everything. But for now, all of us will have to learn how to put up with all of the rest of us because that is what a worthy walk looks like. And we should also do so because the lost world is watching and often completely turned off by how they see Christians behave toward each other.

The third part he covers in having us walk worthy of the vocation we have been called to is that we endeavour *"to keep the unity of the Spirit in the bond of peace."* This clearly ties in with what came right before it. When we see Paul use the word "endeavor" in this instruction, it may give us the wrong idea based on how we normally use the word endeavor in our modern day. We simply think of it as "to try, to give it our best shot." And if we took it that way, we would, first of all, be giving ourselves an out ("I tried, I really did, but that person is just such a donkey's rear end!"), and we would secondly not be being true to the actual meaning of the word. It is from the word *spouday,* and it means "to hasten, to exert oneself, to be diligent about." So, Paul was not so much saying, "Try and see if you can manage to do it," he was saying something more like, "Go do this, and be quick and consistent about it!"

And what was it, again, that he expected from us? *"Endeavouring to keep the unity of the Spirit in the bond of peace."* We are to be quick and consistent and diligent about keeping (guarding, carefully taking care of) the unity of (sourced from and indicative of) the Holy Spirit that now lives within us. And we are to do so "in the bond of peace." The bond means "the ties, what holds us together." And those ties are very specifically peace, meaning the peace that God gives us with Himself and with each other.

Adam Clarke summarized the setting and situation this way:

> "There can be no doubt that the Church at Ephesus was composed partly of converted Jews,

as well as Gentiles. Now, from the different manner in which they had been brought up, there might be frequent causes of altercation. Indeed, the Jews, though converted, might be envious that the Gentiles were admitted to the same glorious privileges with themselves, without being initiated into them by bearing the yoke and burden of the Mosaic law. The apostle guards them against this... (6:451)

I would add, though, that the racial and historical backgrounds were not even necessary for there to be issues with division and strife. The twelve apostles were all Jews, and yet they often fought like cats and dogs, even when Christ was walking among them!

People are people. Even saved people are still people. And people fight. They fuss. They backbite. They hurt each other. And none of it, none of it at all, is worthy of our calling.

A unity that binds us

Paul just got done alluding to a bunch of different people, a bunch of different "moving parts" to the body of the church. Now he will begin to paint all of the parts as they really are: a singular unit from a singular source. And once again, three verses will comprise one long sentence. As we go through them, watch for repeated usages of the word "one" because there will be seven of them in just three verses.

Ephesians 4:4 *There is* **one** *body, and* **one** *Spirit, even as ye are called in* **one** *hope of your calling;* **5 One** *Lord,* **one** *faith,* **one** *baptism,* **6 One** *God and Father of all, who is above all, and through all, and in you all.*

When Paul said, "There is one body," we know immediately that he was not talking about a local church; there were already many more than just one local church. The letter was sent to a local church, yes, but this one body was bigger than just that. Yes, we can rightly call local churches "bodies," but the body Paul was pointing to was the saved, the body of Christ. There is just one of those. This is the start of the unity that binds us; there are not multiple saviors and multiple plans of salvation and multiple tiers of "saved," there is just one body. Whoever is saved is part, and equally part, of that one body.

After telling them that there was just one body, Paul then told them that there is **one** *Spirit*. That is referring to the Holy Spirit. There is no Jewish Holy Spirit and Gentile Holy Spirit and Yankee Holy Spirit and "strang-pickin' " Southern Holy Spirit. There is just the Holy Spirit. The exact same Holy Spirit that lives in me lives in Pastor Michael Lambert in Grenada and in some Iraqi believer in the desert that I do not know and will not meet until we arrive together in heaven.

Paul then said, *"even as ye are called in* **one** *hope of your calling."*

We all have one hope, one exact same hope, that springs out of our calling. There is no Jewish heaven and Gentile heaven and Yankee heaven and "Down by the river with a fishin' rod" Southern heaven. There is just heaven, and all of the saved are going.

Then Paul said that there is *"****One*** *Lord."* There is just Jesus, period. There is no Jesus for the Jews, or Jesus for the Gentiles, or Jesus for Yankees, or Jesus for "yee-haw glow-ry" Southerners. There is just Jesus, and He is Lord of all the saved.

The next one is, in practice, a bit trickier, though not a whit less true. Paul said that there is *"****one*** *faith."* And if that only referred to saving faith, there would not be much of an issue. There undeniably is only one saving faith, faith in Christ. But this word refers not just to that but also to the entire body of doctrine that we are to hold and practice. Jude used it that way when he said that we are to *"earnestly contend for the faith which was once delivered unto the saints."* (**Jude 1:3**).

Whether it looks like it anymore or not, there is no Jewish Christian doctrine or Gentile Christian doctrine or Yankee Christian doctrine or Southern Christian doctrine. Nor is there any Baptist Christian doctrine or Methodist Christian doctrine or Presbyterian Christian doctrine. There is just Biblical Christian doctrine, and we are all just arguing over who is getting it right!

But we are not going to solve that in this verse; this verse just simply lays out the truth for us that we ought to be unified because God gave us exactly one Book and exactly one set of Christian doctrines.

Moving on from the one faith, Paul then said that there is "***one** baptism.*" Once again, there was and is no Jewish baptism or Gentile baptism or Yankee baptism or Southern baptism. Paul did not form two lines in Ephesus and have the Jews in this line to be baptized with spring water and the Gentiles in the other to be baptized in pond water. Everyone got baptized the same way and in the same available body of water and in the same name of the Father and Son and Holy Ghost.

Paul closed the list by saying that there is "***One** God and Father of all.*" You know how it goes by now. There is not a God and Father of the Jews, and a different one for the Gentiles, and a different one for the Yanks, and a different one for Southerners. There is just God the Father, and He is the only God our Father, and He is equally God the Father to all the saved. And that God, as Paul reminds us, is "*above all, and through all, and in you all.*" He is above all; omnipotent and unchangeable. He is through all; omnipresent and active. He is in you all; He is personally dwelling in all of the saved by means of the Holy Spirit.

So, since all of this is true, how could we not be unified? How could we ever be splintered and fractious and schismatic and cliquish?

Barnes put all of this in these eloquent words:

"Christ... did not come to save merely the black man, or the red, or the white man; nor did he leave the world to set up for them separate mansions in the skies. He came that he might collect into one community a multitude of every complexion, and from every land, and unite them in one great brotherhood on earth, and ultimately assemble them in the same heaven. The church is one. Every sincere Christian is a brother in that church, and has an equal right with all others to its privileges. Being one by the design of the Saviour, they should be one in feeling; and every Christian, no matter what his rank, should be ready to hail every other Christian as a fellow-heft of heaven." (Linder)

That is absolutely correct. And if we are not living like it, then we are not engaging in a worthy walk.

Chapter Eleven

Gifts for the Body

Ephesians 4:7 *But unto every one of us is given grace according to the measure of the gift of Christ.* **8** *Wherefore he saith, When he ascended up on high, he led captivity captive, and gave gifts unto men.* **9** *(Now that he ascended, what is it but that he also descended first into the lower parts of the earth?* **10** *He that descended is the same also that ascended up far above all heavens, that he might fill all things.)* **11** *And he gave some, apostles; and some, prophets; and some, evangelists; and some, pastors and teachers;* **12** *For the perfecting of the saints, for the work of the ministry, for the edifying of the body of Christ:* **13** *Till we all come in the unity of the faith, and of the knowledge of the Son of God, unto a perfect man, unto the measure of the stature of the fulness of Christ:* **14** *That we henceforth be no more children, tossed to and fro, and carried about with every wind of doctrine, by the sleight of men, and cunning craftiness, whereby they lie in wait to deceive;* **15** *But speaking the truth in love, may grow up into him in all things, which is the head, even Christ:* **16** *From whom the whole body fitly joined together and compacted by that which every joint supplieth, according to the effectual working in the measure of every part, maketh increase of the body unto the edifying of itself in love.*

After encouraging the believers in Ephesus to walk worthy of their vocation, he will now inform them that they are not simply going to have to pull themselves up by their spiritual bootstraps and do it all in their own power. The God who calls us to a worthy walk also equips us for a worthy walk.

A mystery explained

Ephesians 4:7 *But unto every one of us is given grace according to the measure of the gift of Christ.* **8** *Wherefore he saith, When he ascended up on high, he led captivity captive, and gave gifts unto men.* **9** *(Now that he ascended, what is it but that he also descended first into the lower parts of the earth?* **10** *He that descended is the same also that ascended up far above all heavens, that he might fill all things.)*

When Paul begins verse seven with the word "but," you should know that a correlating yet contrasting thought is about to begin. And in this case, what it correlates to and contrasts with is all of the "ones" of the last few verses that compel believers to unity:

Ephesians 4:3 *Endeavouring to keep the **unity** of the Spirit in the bond of peace.* **4** *There is **one** body, and **one** Spirit, even as ye are called in **one** hope of your calling;* **5** ***One** Lord, **one** faith, **one** baptism,* **6** ***One** God and Father of all, who is above all, and through all, and in you all.*

After using the word unity and after seven times using the word one, Paul then says, "But, by contrast, even though we are to be united in the body, even though we have seven reasons to be in oneness with each other, *"unto every one of us is given grace according to the measure of the gift of Christ."*

Yes, we are one body, but we are also unique individuals within that one body. God is not assembling a hive-mind collective; He is assembling a body of unique individual parts. And unto every single one of us individually He has given *"grace according to the measure of the gift of Christ."*

You are going to find the words grace and giving and gifts scattered throughout these verses. The subject matter of these verses is what God has given us as gifts to be used in and for the body. None of it is earned; verse seven tells us that all of it, just like salvation itself, is grace. And it is not given according as we have earned or even according as we desire; it is given *"according to the measure of the gift of Christ."*

In other words, these gifts He gives to us are of His choosing both in type and in degree.

You really need to grasp that because it is essential to a proper understanding of spiritual gifts. We do not get to pick our gifts; we do not get to choose how filled we are with a gift or gifts; we simply receive these gifts as God chooses and in the measure that He chooses. And that, among other things, is what makes it so ridiculous to focus on tongues or any other gift and make the possession and use of it or them some litmus test for spirituality or for Spirit filling.

Having made all of that very clear in verse seven, Paul will now use verse eight to remind the reader of an Old Testament passage and explain how it is fulfilled in all of this.

Ephesians 4:8 *Wherefore he saith, When he ascended up on high, he led captivity captive, and gave gifts unto men.*

Wherefore (because God gives gifts to men as He sees fit to use in and for the body) he saith *"When he ascended up on high, he led captivity captive, and gave gifts unto men."*

Paul was paraphrasing Psalm 68:18:

Psalm 68:18 *Thou hast ascended on high, thou hast led captivity captive: thou hast received gifts for men; yea, for the rebellious also, that the LORD God might dwell among them.*

This was written a thousand years earlier. It is very unlikely that David, the author of this Psalm, had any idea what it ultimately meant when God gave him the words for it. It would be up to Paul a thousand years later to point out that it was prophetic of Christ and referred to His ascension back into heaven, His taking the saved souls in Paradise into heaven with Him, and Him leaving gifts for the church to use on His behalf in His absence.

He will elaborate on all of that in the next couple of verses. But for now, we should look at one matter before we move on into verse nine, namely what may be mistakenly taken as a contradiction in Scripture.

Look at the two verses in question back-to-back:

Ephesians 4:8 *Wherefore he saith, When he ascended up on high, he led captivity captive, and* ***gave gifts*** *unto men.*

Psalm 68:18 *Thou hast ascended on high, thou hast led captivity captive: thou hast* ***received gifts*** *for men;*

It is easy to see why a careless reading of these passages may draw charges of contradiction; gave and receive are different things. But the last two words of each passage more than sufficiently dispel any notion of error or contradiction. Ephesians 4:8 says he "gave gifts **unto** men." Psalm 68:18 says he "received gifts **for** men." So, in both verses, who ultimately ends up with the gifts? Men. There is no contradiction at all. Both passages simply tell us that Christ gave gifts to men, but Psalm 68:18 adds the additional fact that what Christ gave to men, He first received Himself, obviously from His Father.

Now, clearly, that verse, especially the part about descending and taking captivity captive, was going to make for some wide eyes in Ephesus; that is not exactly something one hears about every day. So Paul used the next two verses to elaborate on that:

Ephesians 4:9 *(Now that he ascended, what is it but that he also descended first into the lower parts of the earth?* **10** *He that descended is the same also that ascended up far above all heavens, that he might fill all things.)*

There are two places and a purpose to be seen and understood in these verses. The two places are where He ascended to and where He descended to, and the purpose is why He did so. As to the places, one of those two is exceedingly obvious, namely, where He ascended to:

John 6:62 *What and if ye shall see the Son of man ascend up where he was before?*

Acts 1:9 *And when he had spoken these things, while they beheld, he was taken up; and a cloud received him out of their sight.* **10** *And while they looked stedfastly toward heaven as he went up, behold, two men stood by them in white apparel;* **11** *Which also said, Ye men of Galilee, why stand ye gazing up into heaven? this same Jesus, which is taken up from you into heaven, shall so come in like manner as ye have seen him go into heaven.*

1 Timothy 3:16 *And without controversy great is the mystery of godliness: God was manifest in the flesh, justified in the Spirit, seen of angels, preached unto the Gentiles, believed on in the world, received up into glory.*

Hebrews 4:14 *Seeing then that we have a great high priest, that is passed into the heavens, Jesus the Son of God, let us hold fast our profession.*

Hebrews 8:1 *Now of the things which we have spoken this is the sum: We have such an high priest, who is set on the right hand of the throne of the Majesty in the heavens;*

So there really is no legitimate controversy on the ascension part; Jesus ascended into heaven. As to the descended part, though, there is a bit of controversy, though there should not be. Many commentators take the position that it simply refers to Him coming to earth. But that is not what the text says:

Ephesians 4:9 *(Now that he ascended, what is it but that he also descended first into **the lower parts** of the earth?*

Earth alone does not get the job done; He descended into the lower parts of the earth. But that brings up another view, namely that it is the grave that is being referred to. And that view might be plausible if we had not been given additional Scripture on the subject:

1 Peter 3:18 *For Christ also hath once suffered for sins, the just for the unjust, that he might bring us to God, being put to death in the flesh, but quickened by the Spirit:* **19** *By which also he went and preached unto the spirits in prison;* **20** *Which sometime were disobedient, when once the longsuffering of God waited in the days of Noah, while the ark was a preparing, wherein few, that is, eight souls were saved by water.*

When we find that Christ, after His death, went and preached to the disobedient spirits from Noah's day who were even then imprisoned for their rebellion, that takes things to a level way lower than the grave. Christ descended all the way into the center of the earth, took a trip to the hell side, preached His victory to the disobedient Spirits, and then vacated the entire Paradise side when He ascended back into heaven, taking all of those Old Testament saints with Him into heaven.

Paul closes out this unique section of verses this way:

Ephesians 4:10 *He that descended is the same also that ascended up far above all heavens, that he might fill all things.)*

Adam Clarke aptly says of this verse, "His abasement was unparalleled; so also is his exaltation." (6:452)

There is a matter of identity that Paul wants to drive home firmly in this verse, and we find it in the words "the same." And in the language that Paul wrote it to the Ephesians, it is equally or more forceful, something akin to "He himself is the same one." Paul wanted to emphasize that it was indeed Jesus that did all of this ascending and descending. It was not the Father; it was not the Holy Spirit; it was not someone else entirely; it was Jesus who did all of this.

It really is all about Him.

And all of it had a purpose. It was, as the last half of the verse states, that, meaning in order that, *"he might fill all things."*

As you might suspect, that is a huge statement with magnificent implications. Jesus did not come to earth and live and die and descend into the lower parts of the earth and ascend back into heaven and take all of Paradise with Him just because He is "nice." He did not do all of this just because He cares. He did not do all of this to make people feel good about themselves. He definitely did not do all of this to leave people and situations and circumstances as they are. He did all of this to *"fill all things,"* not with a what, but with a Who, namely with Himself. In other words, this entire marvelous plan of redemption is going to culminate with everyone and everything in existence being filled *with* Christ and reflective *of* Christ.

If you wonder how eternity is going to be different than things were in the garden of Eden, if you wonder how we can be so sure there will never be a part two of that fiasco, this is how. Yes, earth and the entire universe was perfect in the beginning in the sense of being without flaw. But it clearly was not all filled with Christ. Lucifer very obviously was not filled with Christ. Even Adam and Eve were very clearly not filled with Christ.

But when this entire marvelous plan of God is done, everyone and everything and every circumstance and every place and every time will be absolutely filled with Christ. Not only will there be no sin, there will be no temptation *to* sin or desire *for* sin. There will never be any unhappiness with any of our circumstances or any of God's commandments.

When God does things, He does them big!

A ministry equipped

Ephesians 4:11 *And he gave some, apostles; and some, prophets; and some, evangelists; and some, pastors and teachers;* **12** *For the perfecting of the saints, for the work of the* *ministry, for the edifying of the body of Christ:* **13** *Till we all come in the unity of the faith, and of the knowledge of the Son of God, unto a perfect man, unto the measure of the stature of the fulness of Christ:*

In verses seven through ten, Paul has already mentioned some form of the word give or gifts four times. He has explained that though we are all one and be unified in Christ, Christ has given us all gifts as He sees fit and in the measure to which He sees fit. And Paul will now begin to list some of the gifts that God gave us as He left Earth to go back and be with His Father for an extended period of time before returning for His bride.

Depending on how you take one of these phrases, there are either four or five gifts mentioned in these verses that Christ left us. Mind you, there are other lists of gifts in other passages as well, but let's just focus our attention on these gifts in this text. Look again at verse eleven:

Ephesians 4:11 *And he gave some, apostles; and some, prophets; and some, evangelists; and some, pastors and teachers;*

You should very quickly be able to discern the numerical issue in this verse. You have apostles followed by a semicolon, prophets followed by a semicolon, evangelists followed by a semicolon, and then pastors and teachers followed by a semicolon. The question then becomes, are pastors and teachers two different and distinct gifts or two descriptions of the same gift?

Commentators are all over the board on this. But the simple grammar itself, as well as a correlation with other Scriptures such as 1 Timothy 3:2 and 5:17, seem clearly to make these two words descriptive of one office, that of the Pastor, often referred to as the Pastor/teacher. The Peoples New Testament Commentary puts it this way, "These were not distinct offices. Bishops, or elders, and especially those 'who labored in word and doctrine,' came under this head. A pastor should always be an elder, but it is not certain that a teacher was always an elder." (Linder)

So we are dealing with four distinct gifts that Christ gave to the church as He ascended back into heaven.

The first of these gifts was the apostle. The word here is from *apostolous*, and it generically means "a delegate, one who is sent with a message." But as it is used in Scripture, it has a more specific meaning. These were not just any messengers with any message; these were specifically messengers sent forth by Christ Himself with His message.

There is a bit of an honest debate on the number, but there seem to have been roughly two dozen or so of these in the New Testament. And one of the qualifications given that lets us know that this was a one generation gift:

Acts 1:21 *Wherefore of these men which have companied with us all the time that the Lord Jesus went in and out among us,* **22** *Beginning from the baptism of John, unto that same day that he was taken up from us, must one be ordained to be a witness with us of his resurrection.*

Verse twenty-one is practical; verse twenty-two is precept. By this, we mean that Peter said what he said in verse twenty-one because it was the only logical and viable option at that time, but what he said in verse twenty-two was the entire point of the matter and thus was binding for all time. If verse twenty-one were binding for all time, Paul himself could not have been an apostle since he most definitely did not company with the others while Jesus was alive. So the permanent qualification for an apostle that we find in this passage is that he had to have been an eyewitness of the resurrected Christ. He could not simply have heard of it from others; he had to be able to say, "I saw Him."

Paul, who wrote these words, had the most unique experience in that regard. He saw Him not while he walked on earth between the time of His resurrection and ascension but later on the Damascus Road in a blinding light.

But all of the apostles had to have lived right there in those days and seen the risen Christ in one way or another. They were the foundation of the building, something that would cease to be seen once the structure was up and running. Here, again, is how he put that just two chapters earlier:

Ephesians 2:20 *And are built upon the foundation of the apostles and prophets, Jesus Christ himself being the chief corner stone;*

So the apostle was a one-generation gift, but it was the most powerful and foundational human gift that the church was ever given.

The second gift Christ gave as He ascended, though, was that of the prophet. And that gift had roughly the same shelf life as that of the apostle and right about the same number as well. Depending on how one reckons the list, there seem to have been about twenty prophets listed in the New Testament. Mind you, one half of the ministry of the prophet, that of forth telling, is still applicable for any preacher of the gospel today. But the gift of foretelling, the prophetic ability to know the future in perfection because God told it to you and instructed you to convey it to others, was also a powerful yet short-lived New Testament gift.

Obviously, there are many in our day who take great umbrage to that statement; "prophets" in our day seem to only be exceeded in number by Dollar Generals, and their "merchandise" is usually equal in value to what is found there. But if we are to be true to Scripture, then we must conclude that the clearly given qualifications of a prophet are not at all being met by anyone today, nor are the consequences for failing to meet those qualifications being meted out. Here is the main qualification for a prophet in any age:

Deuteronomy 18:20 *But the prophet, which shall presume to speak a word in my name, which I have not commanded him to speak, or that shall speak in the name of other gods, even that prophet shall die.* **21** *And if thou say in thine heart, How shall we know the word which the LORD hath not spoken?* **22** *When a prophet speaketh in the name of the LORD, if the thing follow not, nor come to pass, that is the thing which the LORD hath not spoken, but the prophet hath spoken it presumptuously: thou shalt not be afraid of him.*

These verses can be summarized in just three words: perfection or death.

Since a prophet was speaking what God told him to speak, perfection was not hard to come by in a real prophet. This is quite a radical departure from the modern pseudo-office of the prophet in which the prophets and prophetesses routinely get things egregiously wrong, knowing good and well that not only will it not be subject to the biblical penalty of death, but their foolish followers will continue to hang on their every driveling word.

After the 2020 presidential elections, with all of its accusations of fraud and lawsuits flying, there was a legitimate question as to whether or not Joe Biden would be inaugurated as the next president or whether Donald Trump would be re-inaugurated as president in January 2020. I watched in wonder as world-famous "prophets and prophetesses," mostly prophetesses, to be fair, proclaimed with great certainty that Donald Trump would indeed be re-inaugurated in January 2020 and serve a full four-year term.

Obviously, that did not happen. Whether it should have happened is not the issue; the fact that it did not happen is the issue. The fact that said prophets and prophetesses did not lose any of their faithful and foolish followers is the issue. Real prophets got it right one hundred percent of the time. And this instilled a sense of awe when anyone heard them speak, a sense of awe the early church desperately needed.

Modern prophets do not instill a sense of awe; they instill a sense of carnival huckster.

But for the early church, the prophet was a great gift from the hand of God until the time that the Scripture itself was completed and the gift ceased of its own accord (1 Corinthians 13:8-10).

The third gift Christ gave to the church on His ascension was that of the evangelist. Unlike the gift of the pastor, which will be mentioned next, the gift of the evangelist was never elevated to the status of a church office/officer in Scripture. The two church officers in Scripture are that of the pastor and deacon. Nonetheless, the evangelist was and still is a powerful and precious gift that Christ gave to the church. Unlike the apostle and the prophet, the gift of the evangelist came without an expiration date.

Not much is said about the gift of the evangelist in Scripture. The word evangelists is only mentioned this once in Scripture, the word evangelist is only mentioned twice in Scripture, and one of those two mentions is an exhortation for Timothy, a pastor, to do the work of an evangelist.

The other mention of evangelist is applied, interestingly enough, to a man who was also a deacon, namely Philip:

Acts 21:8 *And the next day we that were of Paul's company departed, and came unto Caesarea: and we entered into the house of Philip the evangelist, which was one of the seven; and abode with him.*

Clarke says of this, "One of the seven deacons, who seems to have settled here after he had baptized the eunuch." (5:853) Albert Barnes, Jamieson Fausset Brown, John Wesley, Matthew Henry, Robertsons Word Pictures, all are consistent and right in viewing the seven men of Acts 6 as the first deacons and in viewing this Phillip as one of them, as the Scripture clearly states.

Some twenty-five years after we find Philip ordained as one of the first seven deacons, we find him as an evangelist. And as you look over his ministry, the most prominent feature is that he traveled about at God's command, preaching the good news of salvation. It is this Phillip who, in Acts 8:5, went to Samaria to preach Christ, and then in Acts 8:26, he rushed down into the desert to preach Christ to an Ethiopian eunuch.

The word evangelist comes from *euangelistou*, and it generically means "a bringer of good tidings." As it is applied specifically in the New Testament, though, it clearly means "the good news of salvation through the crucified and risen Christ." An evangelist, then, is a preacher, but one who goes everywhere preaching the message of salvation. Where a pastor will be more focused on one location and one body of people and preaching and teaching everything the Bible says, which goes far beyond the message of salvation, an evangelist generally has a wider reach and a narrower scope.

As mentioned earlier, though, there is a bit of an exception to this, or perhaps it would be better to call it a hybrid. Take a look at this:

2 Timothy 4:5 *But watch thou in all things, endure afflictions, do the work of an evangelist, make full proof of thy ministry.*

Timothy was a young pastor and trained as such. But Paul told this particular pastor to also do the work of an evangelist. He did not give this command to anyone else; this leads us to believe that while every pastor should evangelize, some but not all should also do the work of an evangelist. This must therefore be led and directed by the Holy Spirit.

Whether it is done by a pastor or by a full-time evangelist, though, the gift of the evangelist is a powerful and precious one to the local church. God tasked us with fulfilling the Great Commission, and evangelists are uniquely gifted and focused on the soul-winning aspect of the Great Commission. And this helps local churches everywhere to grow and thrive.

The last gift mentioned in verse eleven is the pastor/teacher. Like the gift of the evangelist, and unlike the gifts of the apostle and prophet, the gift of the pastor/teacher is ongoing for today.

The word pastor is mentioned once in Scripture; the plural form, pastors, is mentioned eight times. Of those nine usages, eight are in the Old Testament book of Jeremiah, and only one, this one, is in the New Testament. There are two other words, though, that mean the same thing in the New Testament, the word elder and the word bishop. All three refer to the exact same person and office. In fact, the three terms are actually found together in one place, though you may not realize it.

Acts 20:17 *And from Miletus he sent to Ephesus, and called the elders of the church.*

This is Paul calling specifically for the elders of the church at Ephesus. And it is to those elders that he speaks for the entire rest of the chapter. With that understanding, look at verse twenty-eight.

Acts 20:28 *Take heed therefore unto yourselves, and to all the flock, over the which the Holy Ghost hath made you* **overseers***, to* **feed** *the church of God, which he hath purchased with his own blood.*

I highlighted two words in that verse for a reason. Speaking to the elders, Paul said that the Holy Ghost has made them "overseers." That is from the word *episkopos*. All seven times that you find the word bishop or bishops in the New Testament, it is from that exact word. So Paul literally just said, "Elders, God has made you bishops."

Then we come to the word feed. It is from the word *poimein*, and is the exact word used for pastors here in Ephesians

4:11. So Paul literally just said, "Elders, God has made you bishops, to pastor the church of God."

Understand, then, that pastors and elders and bishops are not three different things; they are three different words for the exact same thing.

As to what this gift entails, the three words for it give us a pretty good picture when put together.

Pastor, *poimane*, is the word for a herdsman, a shepherd. And that fits perfectly with Paul's admonition for these elders to feed the church of God. A pastor is a shepherd who feeds and tends to God's sheep.

Elder is from the word *presbuteros*. It is used generically simply of an older person, and there are times in the New Testament it is applied as such. But when referring to the office and gift of the pastor, it means "a ranking officer, a magistrate, an administrator." It is a term of authority.

Here is a good view from Scripture of how it is to be taken:

1 Timothy 5:17 *Let the elders that rule well be counted worthy of double honour, especially they who labour in the word and doctrine.*

Hebrews 13:7 *Remember them which have the rule over you, who have spoken unto you the word of God: whose faith follow, considering the end of their conversation.*

Hebrews 13:17 *Obey them that have the rule over you, and submit yourselves: for they watch for your souls, as they that must give account, that they may do it with joy, and not with grief: for that is unprofitable for you.*

Notice that word *rule* in every passage. While it is utterly unpopular to say so today, the position of pastor is a position of authority. Someone has to be in charge, and in the church, it is the pastor. Mind you, any real pastor will understand full well that this is a position of a servant leader, not a dictator. Christ taught that explicitly:

Mark 10:44 *And whosoever of you will be the chiefest, shall be servant of all.* **45** *For even the Son of man came not to be ministered unto, but to minister, and to give his life a ransom for many.*

So the gift and office of the pastor is unquestionably the most unique gift of them all. It is a position in which a man is at once in charge of all that goes on but also the servant of everyone that he has charge over.

One year after our annual homecoming service, I put a clearly humorous post on Facebook about the fact that by the time I got to the table, all of the deviled eggs were gone and that I was thinking of having a quick business meeting to address the issue. It never occurred to me that it would actually start a serious conversation about the role of the pastor. A very sweet lady commented that the way she had always seen it done was for the pastor and his family to go first as a sign of respect. I commented back to her that while I very much appreciated that sentiment, and while there was certainly nothing wrong with it, Dana and I have always done it a very different way. From the earliest days, we have always intentionally gone last. For starters, someone almost always needs to talk to us after church. Mostly, though, we have always done that to make sure there is enough to go around for everyone else. I know that I am in charge; that is not an issue. The issue for me is that I want to take care of all of God's sheep really well. And to me, that means putting them first. I do not take issue with any other man or church that does it differently, and I certainly do not think that I am better than any of them. This has just always been my personal choice because I see myself as a servant of all, all the while being in charge of all.

The third word, bishop, is from the word *episkopos,* and it means "an inspector and an overseer." In other words, the pastor is not to hide his face and hope he does not see anything in the church body that needs to be dealt with. He is to actually pay attention and deal with what he sees. This may be among the least popular aspects of the pastorate, both from the one doing it and the ones receiving it! Especially in this generation, people do not want anyone coming to them and telling them, "I noticed this in your life or on your social media or in your work habits or in your relationships, and this really should change, and here is why, Scripturally."

There is nothing in our flesh that likes any of that. But like it or not, it is one of the God-designated responsibilities of a pastor, and it is for our good. A word, though, should obviously be said about how far this extends and to what extent it may be taken. This is clearly all in the context of the local church and the relationship with Christ. The idea that this extends into a pastor snooping into individual lives and homes and micromanaging things that have nothing to do with the church or the relationship with Christ is creepy and unbiblical.

We are not quite through with the gift of the pastor, though, because of the additional word Paul attached to it. Look at it again:

Ephesians 4:11 *And he gave some, apostles; and some, prophets; and some, evangelists; and some, pastors and* ***teachers;***

This is from the word *didaskolos*. Let me show you another place it is used in the New Testament to help you understand it.

Matthew 28:19 *Go ye therefore, and teach all nations, baptizing them in the name of the Father, and of the Son, and of the Holy Ghost:* **20** *Teaching them to observe all things whatsoever I have commanded you: and, lo, I am with you alway, even unto the end of the world. Amen.*

You will notice two references to teach in these two verses. The first one, in verse nineteen is from the root word *mathaytace*, and it means "to make a disciple of," in other words, to win someone to Christ. The second one, in verse twenty, is a completely different word. It is from the root word *didaskolos*, and as you can clearly see from the context, it means "to thoroughly instruct in all the doctrines of the faith."

The first one is about seeing people born into the family of God; the second one is about seeing them grow to spiritual maturity through the teaching of Scripture. And this second one is the same word used in Ephesians 4:11 for the gift of the pastor. Simply put, a pastor is not to be a man whose ministry can be described as a triumph of scream over substance. A pastor is to know how to handle God's word skillfully and thoroughly. He is not just to rally people to shout and run and jump; he is to teach them everything the Scripture says so they will know how to walk.

No matter which one of these precious gifts you are considering, one of the main things for you to understand is that they all were/are for a very specific purpose, a purpose that Paul will begin to explain in the next verse.

Ephesians 4:12 *For* [toward the goal of, for the purpose of] *the perfecting of the saints, for the work of the ministry, for the edifying of the body of Christ:*

Three conjoined purposes for these gifts are given here: the perfecting of the saints, the work of the ministry, and the edifying of the body of Christ.

Let's look at the perfecting of the saints first since it is first on the list. There are different words for perfect or perfecting in the New Testament. This particular one is from the word *katartismon,* and it means "to make completely furnished and equipped." So you can see immediately that it has nothing to do with the salvation of the saint, and everything to do with the person of the saint and everything to do with the provision for the saint. In other words, this is not about salvation; it is about taking one who is saved and properly equipping them for what they will face since they are saved.

When a soldier puts his name on the line and takes the oath, he is a soldier. He is not partially a soldier; he is not sort of a soldier; he is an enlisted soldier. But from then on, he is going to be equipped to be a good soldier. He will be taught how to fight; he will be issued all of the proper gear; those in charge will prepare him for the battles ahead.

These gifts that Christ left us when He went back to heaven are for the exact same purpose spiritually. You could be saved without ever meeting an apostle or prophet or an evangelist or a pastor. But God gave apostles and prophets and evangelists and pastors to help people who do get saved learn and grow as Christians and become thoroughly prepared and equipped for all of the things they will face in their spiritual life. So never forget how relevant and needed pastors and evangelists still are for today. Anyone who stays home rather than becoming a faithful, active member of a local church is, in so many words, saying, "God, I'm way smarter than you are on this subject. Those Evangelists and Pastor/Teachers that you specifically gave to help equip me? I don't need them."

The second reason that Christ left these gifts when He ascended was for *"the work of the ministry."* When we see the words "work" and "ministry" tied together like this, it is a clear indication that Christ left these flesh and blood gifts for them to labor in Christ's service to the body. In other words, apostles and prophets, when those gifts were still in force, and pastors and evangelists even today, should work in the ministry as hard or harder than anyone who works a secular job.

Some years ago, I heard an evangelist state matter-of-factly that he only had a small number of messages and did not intend to put together any more. I could actually give you the exact number, but he has said it often enough that if I did, many people would know who he is, and that is not my intention here. My intention in pointing this out in reference to this verse is to discourage any future evangelists from ever being so lazy.

This gentleman was also quite open about the fact that he would never plunge a toilet or sweep a floor because "he was called to preach, not to do menial tasks." Again, it is nothing but laziness and it is the exact opposite of the pattern Paul laid out here.

I have known pastors who are just about as worthless. But the ministry calls for a much better example than that. A pastor should labor at studying and preparing his own lessons and messages rather than just using material from someone else. He should also work every other facet of the ministry, be it soul-winning or visiting the hurting or, yes, even sweeping the floors or plunging the toilet.

The third reason that Paul pointed out that Christ left these gifts was *"for the edifying of the body of Christ."* Edifying is from the word *oikodomayne,* and it means "building up." And, while seeing the church grow numerically is important and enjoyable, this building up is focused much more on spiritual growth and spiritual strength. If you want to know why God would have you to be a part of a church with a pastor, one of the reasons is so that you can be built up spiritually. A pastor is to evaluate where his congregation is at in regard to holiness and do everything in his power to make them stronger in holiness. A pastor is to evaluate where his congregation is at in regard to their knowledge of Scripture and do everything in his power to help them to know the Scripture better and better every single week. A pastor is to evaluate where his congregation is in regard to their personal walk with Christ and do everything in his power to help them love Christ more and be more like Christ as the days go by.

A pastor that is merely leading a weekly pep rally that leaves his people ignorant of Scripture and carnal in their behavior and nothing like Christ is a failure even if he is pastoring 10,000 people and has written best-selling books.

Ephesians 4:13 *Till we all come in the unity of the faith, and of the knowledge of the Son of God, unto a perfect man, unto the measure of the stature of the fulness of Christ:*

This verse gives us the goal line, as it were, for all of this. Christ left these gifts for these purposes till, until *"we all come in the unity of the faith, and of the knowledge of the Son of God, unto a perfect man, unto the measure of the stature of the fulness of Christ:"*

When Paul mentions here the unity of faith and the knowledge of the Son of God, he is restating what he has already been driving at throughout this book. In so many words, there are two aspects of our Christianity that should be particularly in focus. The first is the unity of the faith, which Paul dealt with extensively in the first half of this book. The unity of the faith is us being in oneness with our brothers and sisters in Christ, with all of us rallying around the faith, meaning both our salvation and the body of doctrine that Christ left for us to follow. The second is the knowledge of the Son of God, meaning our personal understanding of the living God.

God wants us right with each other and having a precise and accurate view of Him, which will then affect every aspect of our behavior.

If we can ever be completely right in both of those things, we will have crossed the goal line of being *"a perfect man, unto the measure of the stature of the fulness of Christ."* That phrase plainly means what it says: if we could ever get both of those things completely right, we would be as perfect as Christ Himself. Obviously, that will never completely happen on this side of Glory. But just as obviously, we should all be striving for it with every fiber of our being, even though we know we will never quite arrive.

But since we never will quite arrive in the here and now, these still applicable gifts that Christ left for us will always be necessary.

A maturity expected

Ephesians 4:14 *That we henceforth be no more children, tossed to and fro, and carried about with every wind of doctrine, by the sleight of men, and cunning craftiness, whereby they lie in wait to deceive;* **15** *But speaking the truth in love, may grow up into him in all things, which is the head, even Christ:* **16** *From whom the whole body fitly joined together and compacted by that which every joint supplieth, according to the effectual working in the measure of every part, maketh increase of the body unto the edifying of itself in love.*

In the last verse, Paul explained that we are to become the "perfect man" in Christ, meaning someone who is fully equipped for the spiritual life. So when we find him beginning in verse fourteen with the expectation that we no longer be children, we know that he is drawing a contrast between those two things; he is giving us an either/or. We can either be immature or mature, ill-equipped or well-equipped, but we cannot be both.

Paul dealt with this exact same issue in the church at Corinth:

1 Corinthians 3:1 *And I, brethren, could not speak unto you as unto spiritual, but as unto carnal, even as unto babes in Christ.* **2** *I have fed you with milk, and not with meat: for hitherto ye were not able to bear it, neither yet now are ye able.*

This was an issue in multiple churches right there in the very first generation of churches, and it is still an issue 2,000 years later. And what is the characteristic of a spiritual child, an immature, ill-equipped believer? They will be *"tossed to and fro, and carried about with every wind of doctrine, by the sleight of men, and cunning craftiness, whereby they lie in wait to deceive."*

The phrase "tossed to and fro" is a descriptive term of a boat out on the sea in high and violent waves. "Carried about with every wind" is a descriptive term of being caught in some violent gust, like a tornado or a hurricane, and blown off of your feet. And the prepositional phrase that follows, "of doctrine," applies to both of those pictures.

This word doctrine is from the exact same root word as the word teacher in verse eleven, the word *didaskolos*. Once again, it means "to thoroughly instruct." But it is very clear from everything that Paul is saying in these verses that it is not good instruction at all! Just like God has His pastor/teachers, the devil also has his own pastor/teachers. And lest you think I am being overly harsh when I say that, look at how Paul put it when he wrote to the church at Corinth:

2 Corinthians 11:13 *For such are false apostles, deceitful workers, transforming themselves into the apostles of Christ.* **14** *And no marvel; for Satan himself is transformed into an angel of light.* **15** *Therefore it is no great thing if his* [Satan's] *ministers also be transformed as the ministers of righteousness; whose end shall be according to their works.*

Paul told the Corinthians that the devil had his own ministers who would pretend to be the ministers of Christ. And that is the exact same thing he was teaching the Ephesians when he spoke of every wind of doctrine and then said, "*by the sleight of men, and cunning craftiness, whereby they lie in wait to deceive.*"

This was and is intentional. False doctrine was peddled then and is peddled now by the sleight of men and their cunning craftiness, men who are lying in wait to deceive the gullible. These are incredibly harsh words; they are also incredibly true and incredibly necessary.

When Paul spoke of the sleight of men, you probably have the phrase "sleight-of-hand" popping into your brain. And you actually should; this phrase referred to carnival-type gamesters who rigged dice and other things in such a way that they would always win, and you would always lose. They are not interested in truth; they are interested in taking what you have.

Cunning craftiness means "to be subtle and skillful in your deception."

What you need to understand from all of this is that the devil is not fighting religion; he is trying to corner the market. If the devil were trying to fight religion, there would be less and less religions and less and less churches as the days go by. But there aren't. There are more religions and more churches and more divergent doctrines than there have ever been. The devil knows that he cannot keep people from exhibiting faith; faith is built into us by our Creator. So he instead focuses on directing people to faith in the wrong thing and faith with the wrong beliefs and practices. And an immature and ill-equipped believer will fall for his poison yet polished ministers time and time again.

Why were Jim and Tammy Baker able to be so successful when they were so obviously hucksters? Because immature, ill-equipped believers are *"tossed to and fro, and carried about with every wind of doctrine, by the sleight of men, and cunning craftiness, whereby they lie in wait to deceive."*

Why was Jim Jones able to get everyone to drink the Kool-Aid? Because immature, ill-equipped believers are *"tossed to and fro, and carried about with every wind of doctrine, by the sleight of men, and cunning craftiness, whereby they lie in wait to deceive."*

Why was it so hard for so many to see through what should have been the obvious red flags concerning Bill Gothard and the Duggars? Because immature, ill-equipped believers are *"tossed to and fro, and carried about with every wind of doctrine, by the sleight of men, and cunning craftiness, whereby they lie in wait to deceive."*

There are so many more examples I could give, many of which are far less famous than the ones above. The point is, God gives these gifts to the church, apostles and prophets in the first generation, evangelists and pastor/teachers in every generation, specifically for the purpose of teaching and training and equipping people to be mature enough not to fall for every new false doctrine that comes round.

Pay careful attention: there is literally an infinite number of potential false doctrines that can be peddled because when you are making things up, there are no limits. But there is only one set of true doctrines, and it is found within the pages of the Bible. And it is the Pastor's job to teach it to you so well and your job to learn it so well that no matter who you hear and no matter how polished they sound and no matter how bright their Colgate smile, if they are peddling error, you will recognize it and get away from it.

Ephesians 4:15 *But speaking the truth in love, may grow up into him in all things, which is the head, even Christ:*

But rather than being an ill-equipped, immature believer, we should be those who are *"speaking the truth in love."* There is error, and there is truth. The devil will have his ministers to peddle the error; all of God's children are to be capable of speaking the truth to combat that error. It is not just the pastor that is expected to be able to do so, it is, clearly, also expected of those that are taught by the pastor, the believers in the pew.

We should find it interesting, though, that Paul chooses this place to tell us to speak the truth in love. It would seem that, since we are trying to combat false teachers and false teachings, since we are wrestling against those who are intentionally trying to deceive, we would get very angry and belligerent in that battle.

But while there are times and places for that, as the rest of the New Testament record clearly shows, the context of this particular issue gives a very good reason as to why, in this case, we would speak the truth in love. You see, we are both pursuing the same audience, we who have the truth and the charlatans who are peddling the error. And if they come across as kind and compassionate and sweet and loving and we come across as mean and hateful and bitter and angry, their error will win over our truth time and time again. Many a pure message has been ruined by a putrid messenger.

Paul goes on to say of those that he expects to speak the truth in love, *"may grow up into him in all things, which is the head, even Christ:"* Once again, Paul is utilizing the picture of moving from spiritual childhood to spiritual adulthood. We are to "grow up" into him in all things. This means that we are to grow into His pattern and His likeness in everything. And, making it very clear who he was talking about, Paul says, *"which is the head, even Christ."* He is the head of this body that is called the church, He is the one who is in charge, and we are to be growing up to be the living picture of Him.

Ephesians 4:16 *From whom [Christ] the whole body fitly joined together and compacted by that which every joint supplieth, according to the effectual working in the measure of every part, maketh increase of the body unto the edifying of itself in love.*

Paul begins to wrap up this section of thought by utilizing the picture once again of a human body and applying it to the church. The church, this body of believers, has one head, Christ, as verse fifteen makes clear.

As a body, Christ makes us *"fitly joined together and compacted."* These phrases mean all of the parts of the body have been properly united and made to coalesce. And when he then goes on to say, *"by that which every joint supplieth, according to the effectual working in the measure of every part,"* it means that every single part of the body functions together for the benefit and smooth operation of the entire body.

If your eyes only sent signals to your brain about things that would impact them, you would stub your pinky toe over and over again. If your nose only functioned to smell the things it likes, you would die for not being able to breathe. If your hand only functioned to benefit itself, you would reach for the lotion all day, every day; you would also starve to death because of that hand never caring enough about the mouth to put food into it.

This is the perfect picture of the church. All of us are to do what we do for the benefit of the entire body, not just ourselves.

A pastor was in a fairly small church and desperately needed someone to sing specials. A man came along who could play and sing, and every service, he would play and sing two specials. And then, one day, the Lord sent several more good singers to the church. So the pastor started having that gentleman sing just one song per service and getting someone else to sing as well. Whereupon he got angry and took his instruments and left.

That is the exact opposite attitude we are to have when it comes to the body. Everything we do is supposed to benefit the entire body, not just the individual doing whatever is being done.

Paul ends this long sentence by saying, *"maketh increase of the body unto the edifying of itself in love."* This decidedly old English phrase means that when everyone does whatever they do for the benefit of the entire body, the body itself helps the body to grow, and it does so harmoniously; it does so in love.

Mature believers are willing to put aside pettiness and smallness in order to see the body grow and grow harmoniously. There is no such thing as a spiritually mature diva; all spiritual divas are immature and incredibly problematic.

God gave gifts for the body so the body could grow and grow harmoniously. Do not be a diva who disrupts that process; be a disciple who drives that process.

Chapter Twelve

Being Gentile Is Okay; Being Like Other Gentiles Is Not Okay

Ephesians 4:17 *This I say therefore, and testify in the Lord, that ye henceforth walk not as other Gentiles walk, in the vanity of their mind,* **18** *Having the understanding darkened, being alienated from the life of God through the ignorance that is in them, because of the blindness of their heart:* **19** *Who being past feeling have given themselves over unto lasciviousness, to work all uncleanness with greediness.* **20** *But ye have not so learned Christ;* **21** *If so be that ye have heard him, and have been taught by him, as the truth is in Jesus:* **22** *That ye put off concerning the former conversation the old man, which is corrupt according to the deceitful lusts;* **23** *And be renewed in the spirit of your mind;* **24** *And that ye put on the new man, which after God is created in righteousness and true holiness.* **25** *Wherefore putting away lying, speak every man truth with his neighbour: for we are members one of another.* **26** *Be ye angry, and sin not: let not the sun go down upon your wrath:* **27** *Neither give place to the devil.* **28** *Let him that stole steal no more: but rather let him labour, working with his hands the thing which is good, that he may have to give to him that needeth.* **29** *Let no corrupt communication proceed out of your mouth, but that which is good to the use of edifying, that it may minister grace unto the hearers.* **30** *And grieve not the holy Spirit of God, whereby ye are sealed unto the day of redemption.* **31** *Let all bitterness, and wrath, and anger, and clamour, and evil speaking, be put away from you, with all malice:* **32** *And be ye* *kind one to another, tenderhearted, forgiving one another, even as God for Christ's sake hath forgiven you.*

Paul spent several verses teaching the church at Ephesus about the spiritual gifts that Christ left to them and to all believers when He ascended back into heaven.

But these were not just any believers that he was writing to; they were a predominantly Gentile church. As such, they had much from their background to overcome in their practical, daily Christian walk. The verses to come, then, will show Paul getting very practical with them and very pointed about their past and the potential dangers that it posed to their present.

A commanded difference

Ephesians 4:17 *This I say therefore, and testify in the Lord, that ye henceforth walk not as other Gentiles walk...*

Let's begin with the "therefore." Paul was alluding back to all of the earlier verses in this chapter and saying, "Therefore, because God expects you to walk worthy, and because He has equipped you to walk worthy through the means of the spiritual gifts that He left to you, therefore do not walk as other Gentiles walk." So this commanded difference that he is giving them is not something that is beyond them; it is well within their reach. In fact, because God has so specifically and generously provided all of these gifts for them, at this point, their walk is a choice, not a chance.

Paul said, I *"testify in the Lord."* This was Paul's way of saying, "What I am telling you now is not my opinion; this is straight from God; it is His desire and His command." So Paul was commanding in the Lord that these saved Gentiles who had been equipped to walk differently than other Gentiles should in fact walk differently than other Gentiles.

Was Paul being racist? Was he stereotyping? Of course not; he was merely stating the obvious. As a whole, the Gentiles of that day were wicked, godless, ill-mannered, and ill-behaved people. And in the verses to follow, he is going to give particular illustration after particular illustration of that fact; he is going to paint them as every bit the dirty and vile people that they were. Think of that, though, in light of our modern hypersensitive age.

For a person, especially a preacher, to negatively broad brush any group is regarded as anathema. And yet Paul did not hesitate to do that very thing, both because it was accurate and because he cared about the Ephesian believers and did not want them to be negatively influenced by those of proven poor character. And this tells us that preachers and parents today should be willing to do the same thing.

If there is a group of young people that are rebellious and disrespectful and wicked, we do not need to tell our children, "Now, be careful around that group; many of them are doing some pretty wrong things, so be sure you look through all of them carefully and try to find the one or two people who might be doing a few right things." No, we need to be saying, "Stay away from those people!"

If there is a crowd our new converts came from that did everything they could to keep them from God, we do not need to be encouraging them to maintain warm relations. Other than evangelistic efforts, we need to be encouraging them to cut the ties.

The world around us has not gotten any more righteous through the centuries. In fact, it has gotten infinitely worse. Paul did not want the Ephesian believers to revert back to their culture; he wanted them to root themselves in their Christianity. And that is the exact same thing that God expects of us today. Believers often have a habit of thinking of themselves in hyphenated terms: American-Christian, Southern-Christian, northern-Christian, black-Christian, white-Christian. But do you see the problem? Every last one of those puts culture before Christian. And every one of those cultures is human, not divine. Every one of those cultures is sinful, not righteous.

The believer must come to the place where culture is what he came *from,* and Christianity is what he has come *to.* The purpose of salvation is not just to get us to heaven; it is to conform us to the image of Christ while still here on earth (Romans 8:29). And that is simply not going to happen unless people are told such unpopular things as, "Don't be like those wicked people; be different."

A corrupt display

Ephesians 4:17b ... *in the vanity of their mind,* **18** *Having the understanding darkened, being alienated from the life of God through the ignorance that is in them, because of the blindness of their heart:* **19** *Who being past feeling have given themselves over unto lasciviousness, to work all uncleanness with greediness.*

Paul now begins to list, verse by verse and line by line, what the Gentile world was like. And he begins with the phrase *"in the vanity of their mind."* And while that phrase sounds almost refined in a sinful sort of way, it is anything but. In fact, it is an incredibly harsh evaluation. Vanity is from the word *mataiotaytee*, and it means "devoid of truth and appropriateness, perverse, depraved, and frail." You would be hard-pressed to find a more brutal evaluation of the mind anywhere in Scripture. And it was then and is now an accurate description of the mind of sinners.

The sinful mind is devoid of truth. In fact, it now goes so far as to deny that there is such a thing as truth.

The sinful mind is devoid of appropriateness. Anyone who doubts that need only spend five minutes at the Pride Parade in New York City and watch full-grown nude men doing unspeakable things in front of children or five minutes listening to people with straight faces defend young women being forced to undress in the locker rooms in front of full-grown men who call themselves women.

The sinful mind is perverse. There is literally no sexual deviancy on earth, including child molestation, that does not have open, unashamed advocates in the public square.

The sinful mind is depraved. It is not that they could understand matters of sin and righteousness but choose not to; it is that they are so far gone that they could not understand such matters even if they would.

The sinful mind is frail. Present them with facts and evidence, and they will respond with screaming and insults and the demand for safe spaces.

It is the vanity of the mind.

The second description that Paul gives the Gentile world is in verse eighteen, all of which goes together to describe one single thing:

Having the understanding darkened, being alienated from the life of God through the ignorance that is in them, because of the blindness of their heart:

The words *darkened* and *ignorance* and *blindness* show the singular thread that runs through this thought. The lost world is blind and in darkness from their head to their heart. This has led to them being *alienated from the life of God,* which refers both to salvation and to the sanctified and sweet life that comes from salvation. And this was not some sovereign, judicial choice of God; it was a free will and fatal choice of man. Albert Barnes very eloquently said of this:

> "The apostle does not say that this was a judicial darkening of the understanding; or that they might not have perceived the truth; or that they had no ability to understand it. He speaks of a simple and well-known fact – a fact that is seen now as well as then – that the understanding becomes darkened by indulgence in sin. A man who is intemperate has no just views of the government of the appetites. A man who is unchaste has no perception of the loveliness of purity. A man who is avaricious or covetous has no just views of the beauty of benevolence. A man who indulges in low vices will weaken his mental powers, and render himself incapable of intellectual effort. Indulgence in vice destroys the intellect as well as the body, and unfits a man to appreciate the truth of a proposition in morals, or in mathematics, or the beauty of a poem, as well as the truth and beauty of religion. Nothing is more obvious than that indulgence in sin weakens the mental powers, and renders them unfit for high intellectual effort." (Linder)

Verse nineteen gives us a Rubicon and the results:

"Who being past feeling have given themselves over unto lasciviousness, to work all uncleanness with greediness."

The Rubicon, the line crossed over in this verse, is that these Gentiles of whom Paul spoke were "past feeling." That two-word phrase is from the word *apailgaykotace,* and it means "to no longer feel pain or grief, to become completely insensitive, to be calloused." This is a moral insensitivity that Paul is pointing to, not a physical one. Sin has a desensitizing effect on a person or even on an entire culture. When people begin to go down the road of sin, it hurts, and they are grieved over it. But after a while, it no longer hurts, and they are no longer sad about it. It progresses to a point where the entire conscience is calloused over, and they are completely insensitive to everything that their sin is causing; they simply do not care anymore.

Notice again what inevitably happens once that line is crossed:

Ephesians 4:19 *Who being past feeling <u>have given themselves over unto lasciviousness, to work all uncleanness with greediness.</u>*

Given themselves over is a pretty frightening phrase. It comes from the word *paradokan,* and it means "to deliver into custody." People who push past the final line, the final warnings in their soul trying to get them to stop, do not find freedom. In fact, they find themselves in bondage to which they handed themselves over. And in this particular case, the bondage is twofold, lasciviousness, and uncleanness with greediness.

Lasciviousness is an old English word that is not used much anymore. And that is a bit of a shame because it is a good and powerful word. It means "unbridled lust, excess, and shamelessness."

Uncleanness with greediness is perhaps one of the darkest and most hopeless phrases in the Bible. Adam Clarke defines it well, saying:

> "This is a complete finish of the most abandoned character; to do an unclean act is bad, to labour in it is worse, to labour in all uncleanness is worse still; but [this is] to do all this in every case to the utmost extent, with a desire exceeding time, place, opportunity, and strength." (6:454)

Taken together, these phrases paint the picture of what the epistle to Romans calls the reprobate mind:

Romans 1:28 *And even as they did not like to retain God in their knowledge, God gave them over to a reprobate mind, to do those things which are not convenient;* **29** *Being filled with all unrighteousness, fornication, wickedness, covetousness, maliciousness; full of envy, murder, debate, deceit, malignity; whisperers,* **30** *Backbiters, haters of God, despiteful, proud, boasters, inventors of evil things, disobedient to parents,* **31** *Without understanding, covenantbreakers, without natural affection, implacable, unmerciful:* **32** *Who knowing the judgment of God, that they which commit such things are worthy of death, not only do the same, but have pleasure in them that do them.*

Romans tells us that God gave them over. Ephesians tells us that they gave themselves over. Both are entirely true at the same time. There comes a point when the line beyond feeling is crossed that the sinner gives himself over to lasciviousness and uncleanness with greediness, and God agrees and gives them over to the reprobate mind they have chosen.

I began to preach revival meetings at a church many years ago. He was there as a little boy, being raised in a godly family, smiling, and being right in the middle of everything.

I was still preaching revival meetings there when he was a teenager; only by then he had become sort of cool and apathetic to the things of God.

And then, he became a young adult and decided that he was a homosexual. But even then, he still defended his Christian family to those who attacked them and told him to hate them.

Later on, though, he savaged his family and broke contact with them.

And then came the day that he reached out to me and told me that he was suicidal and wanted to end his life. I begged him not to do so and told him that we loved him and were praying for him and that everyone would love to see him come home and get right.

But he kept going that direction. And now he is openly mocking God and his family and is utterly unconcerned about sin and consequences. If he has not already crossed the line, he is getting dangerously close to it. And there either will or already has come a point at which he will be unbridled in his lust and shamelessness and will pursue sin to the maximum extent possible until it destroys him.

It is a corrupt display. Sin always eventually leads you to the point of a corrupt display. And this is what Paul wanted the Gentile believers to understand, so they did not ever go back that direction.

A clear discipling

Ephesians 4:20 *But ye have not so learned Christ;* **21** *If so be that ye have heard him, and have been taught by him, as the truth is in Jesus:* **22** *That ye put off concerning the former conversation the old man, which is corrupt according to the deceitful lusts;* **23** *And be renewed in the spirit of your mind;* **24** *And that ye put on the new man, which after God is created in righteousness and true holiness.*

After painting the dire and drastic picture of the filthy and ruined minds of the Gentile world that produces depraved and debauched behavior, it is a blessing that verse twenty starts with the word "but." But, by contrast, *"ye have not so learned Christ."* There is, though, an "if" that goes with the but. Verses twenty-one says, *"If so be that ye have heard him, and have been taught by him, as the truth is in Jesus:"* If we were to rearrange this as our Western minds tend to think, meaning we put the if before the but, the thought would go like this, "If so be that ye have heard him, and have been taught by him, as the truth is in Jesus, ye have not so learned Christ." In other words, if indeed they have truly been saved and truly been taught of Christ, then they have not been taught the wicked ways of the Gentiles by that Christ; they have been taught a radically different and purer lifestyle altogether. Neither the Christ of Scripture nor the Scriptures of Christ instruct or even allow believers to live wicked and unworthy lifestyles. It is not such error and falsehoods of the Gentiles that will be found in Christ; as verse twenty-one instructs, it will always and only be the truth that is found in Christ. And the truth he was referring to, he goes on to spell out in detail over the next three verses.

Ephesians 4:22 *That ye put off concerning the former conversation the old man, which is corrupt according to the deceitful lusts;* **23** *And be renewed in the spirit of your mind;* **24** *And that ye put on the new man, which after God is created in righteousness and true holiness.*

The first truth that Christ teaches us in this passage is that we are responsible for "putting off" the old man. The picture behind that phrase "put off" is that of an individual who is wearing filthy, nasty, horribly smelly clothes, realizes how bad all of it is, and takes all of that garbage off forever.

This is our responsibility, we who are saved. When we get born again, our inner man is completely redeemed. But our outer man is just as lost and wicked as ever. And it is our responsibility to lay all of that aside. Mind you, it is His power working in us that now allows us to do it, whereas formally, we could not, but it is still our responsibility to do so. Those who expect Christ to do all of their daily spiritual bathing for them are every bit as ridiculous as a full-grown adult who still expects mommy to come over and bathe away their daily dirtiness.

We, we the believers, are to put off "*concerning the former conversation the old man, which is corrupt according to the deceitful lusts.*"

The former conversation simply means your old lifestyle. Your old lifestyle as a sinner is corrupt according to the deceitful lusts of your heart. When you were lost, you wanted things you should not have, and you therefore had things you should not have wanted. As a saved person, Christ has taught you differently. You are not to say yes to your old man, your flesh; you are to consistently say no.

But as you might imagine, if this is left simply as a negative proposition, a "thou shalt not," then it is very difficult to maintain over the long term. A life comprised solely of "don't" is a miserable life to even attempt to live, and not likely one that a person will endure for long. And that is why, hard on the heels of all of this "don't," verses twenty-three and twenty-four are such a breath of fresh air.

Ephesians 4:23 *And be renewed in the spirit of your mind;* **24** *And that ye put on the new man, which after God is created in righteousness and true holiness.*

Verse twenty-two tells us about the old, verse twenty-three tells us about the renewed. Verse twenty-two gives us the "put off," verse twenty-four gives us the "put on."

The old man has to go; in its place is to be a new man who is renewed in the spirit of his mind. In other words, we are never to think the way that we did when we were lost. Actions commonly come from thoughts, so when we change the way we think, we normally change what we do.

Verse twenty-four tells us that we are to put on the new man. This is every bit as much a choice of the will each day as putting off the old man. We cannot simply put off the old man and then expect nothing in its place; it will either be the old man or the new, and if we do not intentionally put on the new, we will unintentionally slip back into the old.

Paul describes this new man we are to be putting on this way: *"which after God is created in righteousness and true holiness."* This is a unique way of reiterating what God said in the very first chapter of Scripture, that we are made in His image. God made man to be pure, not putrid; sanctified, not sinful. Day by day we are, therefore, to be behaving on the outside the way that God has remade us on the inside. Our new practice is to match our new position, not simply because wrong is wrong and right is right, but because God is right, and we desire to reflect His glory.

One last thing should be noted in this verse, though, and that is the phrase "true holiness." This is the only place in the Bible that phrase is found. And it is used here as a contrast to the phrase "deceitful lusts" in verse twenty-two. This is Paul's way of pointing out that holiness and truth always go hand in hand, as do deceitfulness and lust. It is as impossible to live a life of holiness and deceit as it is to live a life of lust and truthfulness; it will have to be one or the other, and it will have to be our choice.

A chosen distinction

Ephesians 4:25 *Wherefore putting away lying, speak every man truth with his neighbour: for we are members one of another.* **26** *Be ye angry, and sin not: let not the sun go down* *upon your wrath:* **27** *Neither give place to the devil.* **28** *Let him that stole steal no more: but rather let him labour, working with his hands the thing which is good, that he may have to give to him that needeth.* **29** *Let no corrupt communication proceed out of your mouth, but that which is good to the use of edifying, that it may minister grace unto the hearers.* **30** *And grieve not the holy Spirit of God, whereby ye are sealed unto the day of redemption.* **31** *Let all bitterness, and wrath, and anger, and clamour, and evil speaking, be put away from you, with all malice:* **32** *And be ye kind one to another, tenderhearted, forgiving one another, even as God for Christ's sake hath forgiven you.*

As verse twenty-five begins, we find a wherefore, a tie-in back to what came before it. Wherefore, because of all of these truths, put away lying and speak every man truth with his neighbour, for we are members one of another.

Was the Gentile world notorious for lying and deceitfulness? Absolutely. Was that an excuse for these Gentile believers to revert to that bad behavior? Absolutely not. Just like they were to generally put off the old man, they were specifically not to lie to people anymore, especially not to each other, because they are members one of another. This was Paul putting things back in a church context again; he has already spoken at length about them being a body.

Children of God ought to be honest at all times. But we should be intentionally and especially so with our forever family, the household of faith. In other words, the lost habitually lie to the lost, but the saved should habitually tell the truth to the saved.

Ephesians 4:26 *Be ye angry, and sin not: let not the sun go down upon your wrath:* **27** *Neither give place to the devil.*

The first chosen distinction that Paul gave referred to our truthfulness. This second chosen distinction that he gives refers to our temperament. He tells us in verse twenty-six to be angry. That seems odd, doesn't it, in light of the many passages that speak against anger! And yet, Christ Himself was often angry, as was most every prophet of God ever seen in Scripture.

There are times in which it is a sin to not be angry. There are no times, though, when anger justifies sinful behavior, nor are there times that we are allowed to harbor anger. We are to go to bed with wrath laid aside or not at all. And verse twenty-seven gives us the why of that. Harbored anger, even a right anger directed at a right target, will be used by the devil to gain a bit of topography in our lives. And since there is no good place in your life to allow the devil to pitch his filthy tent, there is no good place in your life to allow harbored anger.

Ephesians 4:28 *Let him that stole steal no more: but rather let him labour, working with his hands the thing which is good, that he may have to give to him that needeth.*

From truthfulness and temperament, Paul now turns his attention to taking. And it is a pretty embarrassing indictment of the Gentile world that Paul had to say these words, especially since he was saying them to believers. He actually had to tell people who were saved not to steal anymore but to go to work instead at some honest job and to use those wages to give to others in need. And yet, how many today still need those instructions! God's command for our lives is that we do not take what belongs to other people and that we work honest jobs and that we pay our own bills and that we give generously to others in need.

Yes, I realize that those simple instructions are now viewed as hate speech by an entire generation of brainwashed university kids who think that Jesus was a socialist and that Karl Marx was a hero. Even in churches across our land, there are a great number of people who have no problem with the concept of theft. But nothing that anyone else has belongs to any of us, even if they are billionaires and we are just "hundredaires." Whether theft occurs at the point of a gun or the point of a fountain pen, whether it is direct or indirect, it is still wicked, and we are still to abhor it.

And whether we have much or whether we have a little, we are still to observe the command to give to those in need. This is, in fact, one of the nicest things about working. Nothing will bring you any greater joy in life than doing for others.

Ephesians 4:29 *Let no corrupt communication proceed out of your mouth, but that which is good to the use of edifying, that it may minister grace unto the hearers.*

From truthfulness and temperament and taking, Paul now begins to deal with the tongue. He gives a command that was necessary and yet embarrassing in his day and equally as necessary and equally as embarrassing in our day. What wretchedness that Christians have to be told not to curse and not to tell dirty jokes and not be filthy in any way in their talk!

This is not a small matter. Christians should never talk in such a way as to bring disrepute to the name of Christ and the testimony of the church. In fact, this is such a serious command that it is written in a unique and almost sadly humorous way. Our English translators naturally did a perfect job of smoothing it out for us and making it understandable. And they needed to because the odd way the Ephesians read it was *"pas logos sapros ek tou stomatos humone may ekporuestho."* That comes out to something like, "All words that are rotten, out of the mouth of you let them never come."

You see why our English Bible has it the way it has it. It is a perfect way to get the fact across to us that God is not okay with us saying one single filthy word, ever, not even a "mild one." The lost world is going to have potty mouths; the child of God is never ever to do so. And the last half of the verse starts with but, from *alla,* a strong adversative, showing that it has to be one or the other. It says, *"but that which is good to the use of edifying, that it may minister grace unto the hearers."*

Filthy talk, corrupt communication is not good. It does not edify; it does not build up; it does not minister grace unto the hearers. But good speech does all of that. And if it does not do all of that, then it is not good speech. Good speech may make you fall silent or laugh or cry or groan, but it will not make you dirty inside. Good speech ministers grace; it "gives good gifts" to the hearers.

From truthfulness and temperament and taking and the tongue, Paul now begins to deal with the temple, the body of the saved, and the One who dwells in it.

Ephesians 4:30 *And grieve not the holy Spirit of God, whereby ye are sealed unto the day of redemption.*

When a person gets saved, the Holy Spirit of God takes up residence inside of them:

1 Corinthians 6:19 *What? know ye not that your body is the temple of the Holy Ghost which is in you, which ye have of God, and ye are not your own?* **20** *For ye are bought with a price: therefore glorify God in your body, and in your spirit, which are God's.*

Romans 8:9 *But ye are not in the flesh, but in the Spirit, if so be that the Spirit of God dwell in you. Now if any man have not the Spirit of Christ, he is none of his.*

This Holy Spirit that dwells in us has sealed us unto the day of redemption. The word for seal here in Ephesians 4:30 means "to set a seal upon for security, to authenticate." This is one of a great many passages in the Bible that clearly teach the doctrine of eternal security. We have not been sealed conditionally or temporarily; we have already been sealed unto the day of redemption. We are authenticated as belonging wholly to Christ.

But the first half of the verse often seems a bit neglected both in theology and practice:

Ephesians 4:30 *And grieve not the holy Spirit of God...*

Since we are no longer our own, the Holy Spirit who lives in us cannot be "evicted." He can, though, be grieved. He can be made sorrowful through what we do and say on a daily basis. And it is interesting to note that Paul did not give any type of a list here of what we should avoid doing in order to not grieve Him. The reason for that is because it is unnecessary since it is stated in His name.

If I told you that the name I had chosen for myself is Bo Ihatecheese, what would you not attempt to serve me for dinner? Hopefully, you would not attempt to serve me cheese! Thankfully, I love cheese, so you are welcome to do so. The point is, when the third member of the Trinity calls Himself "the HOLY Spirit," then it is any and all unholiness that grieves Him. When you or I sin, we are wounding the very One who has been so kind as to seal us unto the day of redemption.

From truthfulness and temperament and taking and the tongue and the temple, Paul now ends this chapter with two verses on tenderness.

Ephesians 4:31 *Let all bitterness, and wrath, and anger, and clamour, and evil speaking, be put away from you, with all* *malice:* **32** *And be ye kind one to another, tenderhearted, forgiving one another, even as God for Christ's sake hath forgiven you.*

A great deal of "putting" has been spoken of from verse seventeen to the end of the chapter. Verse twenty-two instructed us to put off the old man. Verse twenty-four instructed us to put on the new man. Verse twenty-five instructed us to put away lying. And now verse thirty-one instructs us to put away *"all bitterness, and wrath, and anger, and clamour, and evil speaking,"* and then adds *"with* [along with, together with] *all malice."* Clearly, this passage of Scripture is big on the personal responsibility of the believer.

So what are these six things that we are to be putting away?

Bitterness is first, and it is largely self-defining. We are not to harbor a deep, awful sourness in our hearts toward others, especially not for others in the family of God.

Wrath is second, and it means heated passion and rage, a sudden outburst of fury.

Anger is third, and it means a settled condition of anger. Whereas wrath may be quick and done, this anger settles in for the long haul.

Clamor is fourth, and it means shouting at each other angrily. How sad that Paul should have to say such a thing to believers in Christ! But anyone who has been in church for a long period of time has likely seen such "clamor."

Evil speaking is fifth, and shockingly enough, it comes from the same word as blasphemy. It means injurious and slanderous speech directed toward one another.

The sixth item, all malice, a seeming addendum to this list that is not really an addendum at all, means "ill will." It is set aside by itself as a way of making it an umbrella term to encompass everything that has come before it and anything that has not been stated and yet fits under it.

None of these are to be harbored or tolerated or cultivated in our lives; all are to be ruthlessly, habitually, intentionally removed.

Ephesians 4:32 *And be ye kind one to another, tenderhearted, forgiving one another, even as God for Christ's sake hath forgiven you.*

This verse is as soothing as the previous one was scalding. In contrast to what came before, in contradistinction to all the things we are to be putting aside in regard to one another, we are to be kind to one another, tenderhearted, forgiving one another.

Kind is not hard to understand. It is often hard to practice, but not hard to understand. But for the sake of definition, if needed, it means benevolent and good.

Tenderhearted is also very much self-defining. We are not to have hard and calloused hearts toward one another; we are to have tender hearts toward one another.

Forgiving one another is likewise obvious in its meaning. Again, often hard to practice, but not hard to understand. But in this case, since it is the hardest of the three, Paul closes the thought with a reminder: *"even as God for Christ's sake hath forgiven you."*

We were not worthy of forgiveness. But God the Father, for Christ's sake, forgave us anyway. And when Paul uses the "even as" formula to start this phrase, it is from the word *kathos,* and it shockingly means "as, even as, in like manner as, and in proportion of." We are to forgive each other *as* God the Father has forgiven us, *even as* God the Father has forgiven us, in like manner as God the Father has forgiven us, and in the same proportion that God the Father has forgiven us.

The lost Gentiles never behaved that way.

But Gentile believers then and now were and are expected to do so.

Being a Gentile is okay, but being like other Gentiles is not okay.

Chapter Thirteen

As Becometh Saints

Ephesians 5:1 *Be ye therefore followers of God, as dear children;* **2** *And walk in love, as Christ also hath loved us, and hath given himself for us an offering and a sacrifice to God for a sweetsmelling savour.* **3** *But fornication, and all uncleanness, or covetousness, let it not be once named among you, as becometh saints;* **4** *Neither filthiness, nor foolish talking, nor jesting, which are not convenient: but rather giving of thanks.* **5** *For this ye know, that no whoremonger, nor unclean person, nor covetous man, who is an idolater, hath any inheritance in the kingdom of Christ and of God.* **6** *Let no man deceive you with vain words: for because of these things cometh the wrath of God upon the children of disobedience.* **7** *Be not ye therefore partakers with them.*

Following hard on the heels of a lengthy passage encouraging the Gentile believers in Ephesus not to be like other Gentiles, Paul will now maintain that same line of thinking as he continues to drive home the point.

The pattern for the saints

Ephesians 5:1 *Be ye therefore followers of God, as dear children;* **2** *And walk in love, as Christ also hath loved us, and hath given himself for us an offering and a sacrifice to God for a sweetsmelling savour.*

Please remember that throughout the book, the main truth that Paul has been striving to drive home to the believers in Ephesus is that they, even as Gentiles, were not just allowed in the beloved, they were accepted, or as we might think of it "absolutely adored" in the beloved. God had, in fact, predestined that Gentile believers should be on equal plane in the household of faith with all Jewish believers.

Was that an example of spiritual riches? Absolutely. But was it, at the exact same time, an extreme spiritual responsibility? Absolutely once again. So, as Paul begins this chapter, he refers to them in a special way, reflecting both those riches and that responsibility. He tells them to *"Be ye therefore followers of God..."*

When he told them to be "therefore" followers of God, that takes us right back to everything that Paul just got done telling them about how they should not walk as other Gentiles walked, but instead follow the example of Christ. But his next words, *"as dear children,"* put everything in a very special context.

As sad as it may sound, not every child is a "dear child." The word for dear in this phrase is from the famous word *agapé*, and it indicates one who is absolutely beloved. Some children are like that to their parents, and those who are, unless they have seared their own conscience, know it. Some children are not like that at all to their parents, and they also know it. And, in general, a child will respond accordingly. A child with an absentee or abusive parent will tend to behave very differently toward parents than the child who has parents that truly love them and demonstrate it on a daily basis.

A child who is a dear child, a beloved child, will, under normal circumstances, try with all of their might to be like the parent who so loves them. A father who adores his son will likely have a son who tries to walk like his dad, wants to dress like his dad, and pursues the same hobbies and often even the same career as his dad. A mother who adores her daughter will likely have a daughter who adopts the same mannerisms as her mother, wants to look like her mother, and talks like her mother. "Dear children" normally follow their parents. In like manner, those who know that they are dear children of God normally follow God.

And what does that pattern look like? Verse two will answer that question:

Ephesians 5:2 *And walk in love, as Christ also hath loved us, and hath given himself for us an offering and a sacrifice to God for a sweetsmelling savour.*

A moment ago, I told you that the word for "dear" in verse one was from the famous word *agapé*. And now, as we look in verse two, we find that same root word again for the word love. In essence, Paul was saying, "you are loved, so walk in love." And by this point, it should probably not come as a surprise to you that just five words later, when we come to that word "loved," it is once again from that exact same root word *agapé*. Paul is really trying to drive this truth home!

When you put all of that together, the train of thought goes something like this. "You are loved, so walk in love toward God and others in the exact same way and to the exact same proportion and degree that Christ has loved us." And what exactly does that entail?

Ephesians 5:2b *...and hath given himself for us an offering and a sacrifice to God for a sweetsmelling savour.*

Let's begin with the phrase, *"and hath given himself for us."* If anything in Scripture ought to be utterly obvious in its meaning, this phrase is it. Jesus Christ, the very Son of God, robed Himself in flesh and came down to this earth and lived a perfect human life so that He could then go to the cross of Calvary and die in our stead. It was not compulsory; it was not mandated; He did not have to do it. He willingly gave Himself to do it. And He did so as an *offering* and a *sacrifice* to God.

Now, before you simply skim over those two things and lump them together in your mind, I need to point something out. Many of you are probably old enough to remember a silly little song from Sesame Street that went like this:

"One of these things is not like the other, one of these things does not belong, can you tell which one is not like the other by the time I finish this song?"

The two things found in this verse, offering and sacrifice, both belong but are definitely not like the other. And one of them does indeed almost seem out of place until you think it through.

The one that obviously fits is the word sacrifice. It is from the word *thusian*, and it indicates a sacrificial victim for sin. All through the Old Testament, when a lamb was slain for the sins of the people, that is what was happening. And all of that, absolutely every drop of blood that a lamb ever shed for a man, pointed ahead to one thing and to one person:

1 Peter 1:18 *Forasmuch as ye know that ye were not redeemed with corruptible things, as silver and gold, from your vain conversation received by tradition from your fathers;* **19** *But with the precious blood of Christ, as of a lamb without blemish and without spot:*

Revelation 13:8 *And all that dwell upon the earth shall worship him, whose names are not written in the book of life of the Lamb slain from the foundation of the world.*

Jesus Christ sacrificed Himself for us. He became the willing victim of the judgment for our sins.

That second word, though, the word offering, is very different. It is from the word *prosphoran,* and it means "a gift, a thank offering, an expression of gratitude for blessings." We know full well that Christ died as the sacrificial victim on our behalf, but do you realize that He also died as an expression of gratitude on our behalf? And please remember that in Old Testament times, it was the one offering something to God that was expressing the thankfulness. But on Calvary, it was the one offering Himself that was expressing the gratitude! How amazing is it that the One being slain was expressing gratitude for the ones He was dying for to the Father! For thousands of years, the offerer had expressed thanks to the Father through the offering, but now the offering was expressing thanks to the Father for the ones for whom He was offering Himself!

And both of these things He did as "*a sweetsmelling savour.*" Calvary stank in the nostrils of those who died thereon, it stank in the nostrils of the bystanders who inhaled the odor of sweat and blood, but it smelled like the sweetest thing in the universe to God the Father who was watching His beloved Son do what no one else ever could do if they would or ever would do if they could.

But please remember something: this is about Christ, but in context, it is also about us. All of this started with Paul saying, "*Be ye therefore followers of God,*" and then describing what Christ did for us. So what he is driving at is not just a reminder that Christ did all of this out of His great love for us; it is also a reestablishment of the fact that we are to treat others with that exact same measure of love.

Christ is to be the pattern of behavior both for believing Jews and believing Gentiles, and equally so.

The purity of the saints

Ephesians 5:3 *But fornication, and all uncleanness, or covetousness, let it not be once named among you, as becometh saints;* **4** *Neither filthiness, nor foolish talking, nor jesting, which are not convenient: but rather giving of thanks.* **5** *For this ye know, that no whoremonger, nor unclean person, nor covetous man, who is an idolater, hath any inheritance in the kingdom of Christ and of God.* **6** *Let no man deceive you with vain words: for because of these things cometh the wrath of God upon the children of disobedience.* **7** *Be not ye therefore partakers with them.*

Verses one and two gave us the positive side of the "sainthood" coin. Verses three through seven will flip the coin over to give us the negative side of that exact same coin.

Ephesians 5:3 *But fornication, and all uncleanness, or covetousness, let it not be once named among you, as becometh saints;* **4** *Neither filthiness, nor foolish talking, nor jesting, which are not convenient: but rather giving of thanks.*

These two verses make up one sentence. And they are a list with an essential hinge phrase right in the middle. So let us examine that hinge phrase first, the phrase "As becometh saints." Everything before it and everything after it is something that is not "becoming of saints."

This phrase means as is appropriate for those who are saints. Simply put, based on our royal station, some things are appropriate for us, and some things are absolutely not ever appropriate for us. Some things do not fit with who we are in Christ.

Paul begins by saying, *"But fornication, and all uncleanness, or covetousness, let it not be once named among you."*

Fornication is first on the list, and as in Galatians 5:19, it is from the word *porneia*, and not surprisingly, we get our word pornography from it. Fornication is an umbrella term that encompasses all forms of sexual impurities. Adultery and premarital sex and sodomy and bestiality and lesbianism and pornography all fall under the heading of fornication. Simply put, any sexual gratification outside of the bonds of marriage between a man and his wife is fornication.

Uncleanness is next on the list here, just like it was next on the list in Galatians 5 as well. It comes from the word *akatharsia*. You may recognize our English word catharsis in that word. Catharsis is a purging or cleansing. When you put the a, the alpha privative in Greek, ahead of it, you get the opposite. Uncleanness simply means "living a dirty life in a moral sense."

The next item on the list is covetousness. It is from the word *pleonexia*. It means "greediness, an insatiable desire for more, especially that which others have."

Paul says of all of these things, "*Let it not be once named among you.*" That is a pretty unique phrase. In essence, it means that we are to live our lives in such a way that if we are honestly examined, no one can ever look at us and say, "Those people are fornicators," or "That guy is unclean morally," or "That family over there is covetous." Our reputations are to be so spotless that nothing like that can ever be said of us so much as one single time.

This was Paul's command to a church, a church made up of a whole bunch of different people and a whole bunch of different families! And Paul said, "Let none of this even once be named among you."

We have a high responsibility both to the God who redeemed us and to our Christian family who has been redeemed along with us. We carry His reputation with us in everything that we do, and we carry one another's reputation with us in everything that we do, and all of us carry the church's reputation with us in everything that we do. Because of that, we are to be pure. Not just positionally pure in Christ but personally pure in daily practice.

But the list does not end with those first three items; it continues on into verse four.

Ephesians 5:4 *Neither filthiness, nor foolish talking, nor jesting, which are not convenient: but rather giving of thanks.*

The "neither" that begins this verse anchors it back to the *"let it not be once named among you, as becometh saints"* of the previous verse.

Just like we are not to let fornication or uncleanness or covetousness ever be named among us, we are also never to let filthiness be named among us. That is from the word *aiskrotace,* and it means "that which is obscene or indecent."

It will be readily obvious to anyone with at least one functioning eye and two functioning brain cells that we are living in an obscene and indecent world. Three and four-year-old children are cursing worse than forty-year-old sailors of a bygone era. Men are parading their naked crotches and posteriors in front of children in "pride" parades. Women are wearing so little clothes in public that the entire fabric content wouldn't make a suitable hammock for an emaciated inchworm.

But though the world is filthy, God's people are never to have filthiness named so much as a single time among them. We are not to be obscene; we are not to be indecent; we are to be modest and holy and reflective of the glory of the God who made us and redeemed us.

Foolish talking is next on the list. It is from the word *morologia,* and it means "senseless and stupid words." And while that may seem like such a small matter, please remember that it occurs in the exact same forbidden list as things like fornication and filthiness!

This word does not occur anywhere else in the New Testament. But it was important enough to God and to Paul to have it included here. God's people are to be sensible and intelligent in their words. We are not simply to run off at the mouth and make God look bad by our ignorance.

The next word is also an issue of the tongue, the word "jesting." It is from the word *eutrapalia,* and it means "vulgar, dirty, and coarse talk, especially in joking."

The "dirty joke" has been a staple of human talk for millennia, and there has never been a single instance of it throughout all of those millennia that God has approved of. This kind of thing is never to be named so much as a single time among the saints.

After giving this list, filthiness, foolish talking, jesting, Paul describes these three particular things as things *"which are not convenient."*

When we think of the word "convenient" in our modern day, we think of it in terms of "handy and easy." But that is not at all what this particular word means. It is from the word *anaykonta,* which means "proper, right, and appropriate." Things that are obscene and indecent, words that are senseless and stupid, jokes that are filthy and vulgar, are never, ever "convenient" or appropriate for a dear child of God, and they should never be once named among us.

But verse four is still not quite done yet. The immediate list of wrong is done, but Paul still wants to introduce a pretty strong contrast for us to consider at this point. And that is why verse four ends with the words *"but rather giving of thanks."*

"But" is from the word *alla*, which is always used to point out a very strong, radical contrast. And when you add the word "rather" to it, which here is from the word *mallon,* it gets even stronger. It indicates something along the lines of "but way extremely on the other side of things."

In other words, rather than having these wicked things named among us, rather than having this type of obscene behavior associated with us, rather than having such stupid or vulgar words come out of our mouths, we should be way extremely on the other side of things giving thanks.

People who are obscene and vulgar and foolish are not going to be truly thankful people, and truly thankful people are not going to be obscene and vulgar and foolish. Those two different conditions are as separate as dark and light. So in a practical sense, if you are struggling with filthiness or senseless talk or vulgarity, if you will spend your days constantly and consistently being thankful and expressing thanks, especially for our holy God, then you will find yourself no longer marked by filthiness or senseless talk or vulgarity.

But Paul is not just going to leave us at "do this but don't do the other," he is going to immediately give us some strong motivation to help us with the battle.

Ephesians 5:5 *For this ye know, that no whoremonger, nor unclean person, nor covetous man, who is an idolater, hath any inheritance in the kingdom of Christ and of God.*

Let's examine the meaning of this verse first and then give the application that Paul is making through it. Paul told the Ephesians that they knew something. So he was not about to teach them some new thing; he was about to refer them back to something with which they were already well acquainted. And what they knew was that *"no whoremonger, nor unclean person, nor covetous man, who is an idolater, hath any inheritance in the kingdom of Christ and of God."*

Please notice, as is so often the case with lists of sin in Scripture, that Paul does not deal with activity here, but with identity. He does not say, "No person who commits the sin of the whoremonger," he says, "No whoremonger." He does not say, "No person who does something unclean," he says, "No unclean person." He does not say, "No one who covets," he says, "No covetous man." So he is not dealing with people who slip into sin or are tripped into sin; he is dealing with those living a lifestyle of sin.

No whoremonger has any inheritance whatsoever in the kingdom of Christ and of God. The whoremonger, the person who either prostitutes his body or habitually seeks out sexual sin, does not get to go to heaven.

No unclean person has any inheritance whatsoever in the kingdom of Christ and of God. The unclean person, the person who lives a dirty life in a moral sense, does not get to go to heaven.

No covetous man who is an idolater has any inheritance whatsoever in the kingdom of Christ and of God. The covetous man who is an idolater, the person whose God is gain, does not get to go to heaven.

That is the simple and obvious meaning of this verse. But now we need to figure out how Paul was applying it. And the way to figure that out is by noticing the very first word of the verse, the word "for." That word sends us back to the main thought that came before it, namely that Christians are to be behaving "as becometh saints." So Paul was not trying to tell them that they were at risk of going to hell. He was telling them not to live like those who are going to hell! He was pointing out how very inappropriate it is for those who are on the way to heaven to behave like those who are on the way to hell.

The last two verses need to be taken together to wrap up the thought in the right way.

Ephesians 5:6 *Let no man deceive you with vain words: for because of these things cometh the wrath of God upon the children of disobedience. 7 Be not ye therefore partakers with them.*

When Paul said, "*Let no man deceive you with vain words*," he said it in such a way as to indicate that it was already actually happening. There were already people deceiving the Ephesians into believing that they could live like the lost with no consequence. And Paul wanted them to stop being deceived by such vain, empty, truthless words. Scripture is replete with promises that we will reap what we sow; we will experience the consequences of our own actions in one way or another.

Paul said, "Because of these things, these common sins of the Gentiles that I just mentioned, the wrath of God comes on the children of disobedience."

Children of disobedience is a pretty interesting moniker. When someone in Scripture is described as children of something or sons of something, it means that that something is their main characteristic; it is what defines them. So again, this is not just a trip or slip; this is a lifestyle. It is an indication that when people habitually do what they do, it is because they are what they are.

And when what they are is the children of disobedience, God sends His wrath on them. And Paul did not want the Ephesians to keep on being "partakers with them" in their sin and experiencing God's wrath.

It was already happening. Believers were already getting mixed up with sinners and their habitual sin. Believers on the way to heaven were already experiencing the wrath of God alongside of people who were on their way to hell. That is a stupid and miserable way to live, and it was and is unbecoming of saints.

Notice a few rules with me, please. They apply to the royal family in England. There are a great many of them, but here are a few interesting ones.

When the king or queen stands, everyone in the family stands.

No one can eat after the king or queen has finished his or her meal.

Bowing and curtsying is a requirement. Men of the royal family perform a neck bow, while women curtsy when greeting the King or Queen.

Public displays of affection are looked down upon, especially while traveling. The royal family even refrain from holding hands.

According to the Royal Marriages Act of 1772, royal descendants must seek the monarch's approval before proposing.

A royal wedding bouquet must contain myrtle.

They aren't allowed to vote or even speak publicly about politics.

Monopoly is a forbidden board game.

The royal family must adhere to a strict dress code. The dress code is modest, and no members are seen in casual clothing.

Women must wear hats to all formal events.

The family must accept gifts. They are required to graciously accept the many gifts they are given on a regular basis, no matter how bizarre.

It's considered unladylike to remove a coat in public. So if a royal family member wears one to an engagement, it must stay on the entire time.

The family is expected to learn multiple languages.

You cannot turn your back on the King or Queen. After a conversation with the monarch has ended, he or she is the first to leave—no one is allowed to turn their back to him or her.

Even the children are expected to be graceful. As soon as children are born into the royal family, they are immediately groomed to both wave and speak gracefully.

Women are expected to sit a certain way. The options are legs crossed at the knee or ankle.

Natural makeup is preferred. You won't see a royal dying their hair bright pink or playing around with a bold smokey eye. The palace prefers that royal women wear natural-looking hair and makeup for public appearances.

Cleavage isn't a part of the royal dress code. (Buddemeyer)

You say, "Those are stupid rules!" Well, to a lot of people, they probably are. But you see, true royalty tends to hold themselves to a much higher standard than others, if nothing else, to always help them remember who they are and to set the highest possible example of behavior for others.

And all of them are nothing more than earthly family members of an earthly monarchy. The believers in Ephesus, and you and I today, are literally members of the royal family in heaven, the eternal monarchy.

If anyone ought to have extremely high standards of behavior, it is us.

Chapter Fourteen

As Different as Day and Night

Ephesians 5:8 *For ye were sometimes darkness, but now are ye light in the Lord: walk as children of light:* **9** *(For the fruit of the Spirit is in all goodness and righteousness and truth;)* **10** *Proving what is acceptable unto the Lord.* **11** *And have no fellowship with the unfruitful works of darkness, but rather reprove them.* **12** *For it is a shame even to speak of those things which are done of them in secret.* **13** *But all things that are reproved are made manifest by the light: for whatsoever doth make manifest is light.* **14** *Wherefore he saith, Awake thou that sleepest, and arise from the dead, and Christ shall give thee light.* **15** *See then that ye walk circumspectly, not as fools, but as wise,* **16** *Redeeming the time, because the days are evil.*

In this latter half of the book of Ephesians, Paul has been dealing extensively with the practical, day-to-day life of a Christian, life that is expected to be as practically pure on the outside as it is positionally pure in Christ. He will continue in that same line of thinking in the verses before us, utilizing the perfect picture of light and darkness that is seen so often in Scripture in regard to this topic.

A contrast between light and dark

Ephesians 5:8 *For ye were sometimes darkness, but now are ye light in the Lord: walk as children of light:* **9** *(For the fruit of the Spirit is in all goodness and righteousness and truth;)* **10** *Proving what is acceptable unto the Lord.*

When you see the word "for" in Scripture, treat it in much the same way as you do the word "therefore," and find out what it is there for. This word in this verse ties the truth of verse eight back to the command of verse seven that we be separate from the children of disobedience.

Now, the way Paul phrases this word picture in verse eight is pretty unique. He says, *"ye were sometimes darkness, but now are ye light in the Lord."* When we see light and darkness used as a word picture in the Bible, normally we see a picture in which there is us and the light, and us and the darkness. But in this case, we either are or were that light or darkness!

Paul told his beloved believers in Ephesus that they "were sometimes darkness." It is not just that they walked in darkness; it is that they were darkness, they were defined by darkness, they themselves produced darkness. But when they got saved, all of that changed. Now, he said, "You are light in the Lord." As a believer, it is not just that we walk in the light; it is that we are light, we are defined by light, and we ourselves produce light. Jesus Himself said much the same thing:

Matthew 5:14 *Ye are the light of the world. A city that is set on an hill cannot be hid.*

You say, "But I thought that Christ was the light of the world!" Yes, He did say that:

John 8:12 *Then spake Jesus again unto them, saying, I am the light of the world: he that followeth me shall not walk in darkness, but shall have the light of life.*

But then He went on to say this:

John 9:5 *As long as I am in the world, I am the light of the world.*

Christ is not physically present in the world to be its light today. But we are. So He, the Light, put His candle as it were to our candles and made us the light in His place. None of us will ever be as magnificent a light as Him, but when all of us shine the light that He gave us, together we can light this world up.

As verse eight ends, Paul makes a very pointed contrast for us:

Ephesians 5:8 *...walk as children of light:*

Now drop back and compare that with the last phrase of verse six:

Ephesians 5:6 ...*the children of disobedience.*

Remember that when someone in the Bible is described as the son of something or the child of something, that something is their chief and defining characteristic. So, as lost people, we used to be the children of disobedience. Disobedience to God was our defining characteristic. But now, as saved people, we are the children of light, and we are to walk in that light; we are to demonstrate it as our chief characteristic. And the fact that light and disobedience are contrasted is an intentional punch to the gut to anyone who claims to be walking in God's light while living in disobedience to His Word.

Very quickly, look at verses nine and ten together, and then we will separate them.

Ephesians 5:9 *(For the fruit of the Spirit is in all goodness and righteousness and truth;)* **10** *Proving what is acceptable unto the Lord.*

The reason I wanted you to look at those two together is to point out to you that verse nine is a parenthetical thought. So in your mind, you need to consider verses eight and ten together to see the uninterrupted thought:

Ephesians 5:8 *For ye were sometimes darkness, but now are ye light in the Lord: walk as children of light:* **10** *Proving what is acceptable unto the Lord.*

Prove is from the word *dokimadzontes*, and it means "to prove, test, discover, and demonstrate." And it is that last part of the definition, demonstrate, that is particularly relevant to this context. You see, if we are walking as children of light, if we are being the light of this world that Christ left us to be, then we are demonstrating to the world what is right. It is entirely true that many people who will never read a Bible will read you. You and I are to be walking demonstrations of the Word. If they see it in us, they should assume that it is acceptable unto the Lord.

That is obviously a huge responsibility and never to be taken lightly. If you do not want people assuming that something you say or do is acceptable to God, then do not say it or do not do it.

Now let's go back and look at that parenthetical thought before we move on.

Ephesians 5:9 *(For the fruit of the Spirit is in all goodness and righteousness and truth;)*

As he did in his letter to the Galatians, Paul mentions the fruit of the Spirit here to the Ephesians. And while he does not recount the entire list given there, he does give a good summary when he says that the fruit of the Spirit is in all goodness and righteousness and truth.

If anything in our lives rightly falls under the category of goodness and righteousness and truth, the fruit of the Spirit is in that, He has produced it as we have allowed Him to do so. And this obviously is another way of describing the deeds of the light that Paul has been mentioning in the verses all around this one.

A call to separation and reproof

Ephesians 5:11 *And have no fellowship with the unfruitful works of darkness, but rather reprove them.* **12** *For it is a shame even to speak of those things which are done of them in secret.* **13** *But all things that are reproved are made manifest by the light: for whatsoever doth make manifest is light.*

Paul continues talking about light and darkness in these verses. And the way he begins this section is with words that, truthfully, even a great many weak and carnal saved people do not like even a little bit. He opens this section of verses by commanding us not even have fellowship with the unfruitful works of darkness, and since works can only come from people, this is a command that we separate from the people who are producing those dark and unfruitful works.

It is a command, by the way, that he gave to a great many different people to whom he preached or wrote. Here are a few of those instances:

2 Corinthians 6:14 *Be ye not unequally yoked together with unbelievers: for what fellowship hath righteousness with unrighteousness? and what communion hath light with darkness?*

2 Corinthians 6:17 *Wherefore come out from among them, and be ye separate, saith the Lord, and touch not the unclean thing; and I will receive you,* **18** *And will be a Father* unto you, and ye shall be my sons and daughters, saith the Lord Almighty.

2 Thessalonians 3:14 *And if any man obey not our word by this epistle, note that man, and have no company with him, that he may be ashamed.*

Romans 16:17 *Now I beseech you, brethren, mark them which cause divisions and offences contrary to the doctrine which ye have learned; and avoid them.*

But not only did he command that we not have fellowship with the unfruitful works of darkness, he went on in verse eleven to say, *"but rather reprove them."* In other words, it is not even enough that we just avoid them; it is only enough when we go so far as to reprove them. And that is a strong word that means "to convict, to refute, to severely chide and admonish."

I understand full well the fear that wells up in people's hearts when they hear something like this. Are we to be running around investigating the deep and hidden sins of others and chewing them out for what we find? Are we to be eternal scolds and noodges that no one wants to be around?

Nothing in Scripture bears that out; people actually wanted to be around Christ.

But nothing in Scripture bears out the modern picture of so-called Christianity either, the Christian who fits in so well with this world that people feel comfortable sinning around them. The very same Christ who said, "Come unto me all ye that labor and are heavy laden, and I will give you rest," also said such things as "go, and sin no more," and "except ye repent, ye shall all likewise perish."

Jesus never did go around looking for the wrong things that people were doing. But He also never hesitated to confront and rebuke all of the wrong things that He saw. The fact of the matter is, there really is not much of a need for us to go looking for wrong these days; it is everywhere, open, overt, loud, and proud. And we ought to be just as loud and consistent in rebuking sin as the lost world is in promoting sin.

Paul was pretty serious about this. Look how he phrased it in verse twelve:

Ephesians 5:12 *For it is a shame even to speak of those things which are done of them in secret.*

He said, "It is a shame," meaning base and dishonorable and embarrassing, to even speak of, to have casual conversations about the things which are done by the lost world in secret.

God's people often get so enamored with lost movie stars and lost pop stars and lost country stars and lost reality stars. More than once, I have heard saved people discussing lewd television reality shows, oblivious to what they were promoting. More than once, I have seen believers click like or put smiley faces or hearts on social media posts that were openly promoting wickedness in a person's life. Christians take this matter of the impurity of sin far too lightly.

Ephesians 5:13 *But all things that are reproved are made manifest by the light: for whatsoever doth make manifest is light.*

This is a marvelous illustration utilized by Paul. No matter what you see, whether it is a bolt deep in an engine that you need to remove, or a bird's nest in the attic, or makeup on a lady's face, or the stars in the sky, you can see them for exactly one and the same reason: light. Everything you see, you see because of light.

This verse tells us that all things that are reproved, all things that are to be convicted and refuted and chided and scolded, are made manifest, exposed by the light. Whatever makes things visible for what they really are is light. So on the days that you feel bad for seemingly always having something negative to say about the wickedness of the world around you, remember that light simply does what it does. The light is not responsible for what it reveals; it simply shows what is already there so that people will know what to do about it.

A command to awake and walk right

Ephesians 5:14 *Wherefore he saith, Awake thou that sleepest, and arise from the dead, and Christ shall give thee light.* **15** *See then that ye walk circumspectly, not as fools, but as wise,* **16** *Redeeming the time, because the days are evil.*

Verse fourteen begins with a bit of a mystery that we need to clear up, namely, where does this particular quote that Paul is giving come from? Right off the bat, let me tell you that there is no Old Testament Scripture that it clearly corresponds to.

The beginning of the unraveling of this mystery is found in the word "he." If we find out who that he is, we are on our way to getting things cleared up. And the nearest he in the context of this passage is the Lord in verse ten. In other words, this is not a reference to an Old Testament Scripture; it is a revelation of God to Paul for the New Testament. Paul was saying, "The Lord says, '*Awake thou that sleepest, and arise from the dead, and Christ shall give thee light.*'"

With that cleared up, start back with me at the word wherefore. Wherefore, because of the truth of verse thirteen that "*all things that are reproved are made manifest by the light: for whatsoever doth make manifest is light,*" the Lord says, "*Awake thou that sleepest, and arise from the dead, and Christ shall give thee light.*"

Some very good men and very good commentaries view this as being a command to the lost, those who are dead in trespasses and sins, to get saved. I disagree with that view. The context of this passage is not of lost people who need to get saved but of saved people who need to start living on the outside like the change that has taken place on the inside. Yes, sleep in Scripture is often used as a euphemism for death, be it physical or spiritual. But it is also used as a euphemism for Christians who are not awake and alert and vibrant for the Lord. Paul used it in that exact same manner when he wrote to the Romans:

Romans 13:11 *And that, knowing the time, that now it is high time to awake out of sleep: for now is our salvation nearer than when we believed.*

So Paul is dealing once again with the need for the Ephesian believers to be shining the light all around them from the light source that is within them. And sleeping Christians are not light-shining Christians. Sleeping Christians are dead to the impact that they are supposed to be having on the world around them. And that fits perfectly with the two verses that Paul followed verse fourteen up with:

Ephesians 5:15 *See then that ye walk circumspectly, not as fools, but as wise,* **16** *Redeeming the time, because the days are evil.*

All of this ties together. A spiritually sleeping Christian, a believer who is not acting as a light source to a world dying in the darkness of sin, is walking like a fool. God's command, therefore, is that we walk circumspectly, wisely.

Circumspectly is an excellent old English word. It comes from the word *akribose,* and it means "accurately, with great care." All of us as believers are to be the exact opposite of haphazard and random in our Christian walk. We are to get up planning our day as a Christian and then walk in that plan step-by-step until we pillow our head that night. We are to leave nothing to chance; a believer hoping for a "lucky day" in the Christian life will be sorely disappointed and have a flickering light at best.

When Paul closed this section of thought with the words, *"Redeeming the time, because the days are evil,"* he used a very precious and powerful word for redeeming, the word *exagoradzo.* In this context, it means "to buy something up with zeal and enthusiasm and to use it to its maximum potential."

Here is a number for you: 31,536,000. Do you know what it represents?

Here is the answer. That is how many seconds you had in this year when it began. How many are you down to now as you read this book? And how many years of 31,536,000 have already come and gone for you?

In this life, we have nothing more precious than time. And because the days are evil (and they very much are), we are to be more diligent than ever to use all of our time as wisely as possible. And in the context of this passage, that means to walk right so that you can shed light.

People have used the phrase "as different as day and night" for longer than any of us could possibly know, and for good reason.

During the day, we can see the sun but no stars. During the night, we can see the stars but no sun.

During the day, the earth is warm. During the night, the earth is cool.

During the day, the world itself is pretty noisy. During the night, the world itself is pretty quiet.

During the day, people do. During the night, people dream.

During the day, there are dust bunnies under the bed. During the night, there are monsters under the bed.

Day and night just are not alike, not even a little bit. And believers and the lost world around them are not alike, not even a little bit. And for their part, the lost world gets this. The lost world generally is not guilty of behaving like the saved are supposed to. But the saved are often guilty of behaving like the lost world does.

Let's be as different as night and day, and always on the "day" side of things.

Chapter Fifteen
Of Submission and Spirit Filling

Ephesians 5:17 *Wherefore be ye not unwise, but understanding what the will of the Lord is.* **18** *And be not drunk with wine, wherein is excess; but be filled with the Spirit;* **19** *Speaking to yourselves in psalms and hymns and spiritual songs, singing and making melody in your heart to the Lord;* **20** *Giving thanks always for all things unto God and the Father in the name of our Lord Jesus Christ;* **21** *Submitting yourselves one to another in the fear of God.*

In the previous section of verses, utilizing the familiar picture of the difference between day and night, Paul drove home to the Ephesian believers the need to be walking as the children of light and walking away from the children of darkness. And now he will begin to give, among other things, a power source to energize that command and a plan to execute that command.

A matter of perception

Ephesians 5:17 *Wherefore be ye not unwise, but understanding what the will of the Lord is.*

The "wherefore" of verse seventeen ties back to the statement of verse sixteen that the days are evil. Because the Ephesian believers were living in evil days (and how much more evil are our own days!), they were to avoid being unwise, but by contrast, were to understand what the will of the Lord is.

That first phrase, "*be ye not unwise,*" is really pointed. It comes from the phrase *may ginesthe aphronays,* and it means "don't be like madmen," or as we may put it in our vernacular, "don't be like a bunch of brainless lunatics." It is a derogatory phrase, and in this case, needfully so. In evil days, we do not need to be soft and timid about this. To walk as the children of darkness is the same thing as being a spiritual lunatic, and God expects better of us. So much so, in fact, that the contrasting word "but" that comes next is from *alla,* that word of incredibly strong contrast. In other words, it is a stark either/or. We either understand what the will of the Lord is and act accordingly, or we must regard ourselves as worthy of being committed to an insane asylum.

How perfectly does that fit with our modern day!

A man just won the Miss Netherlands contest. (Gannett)

In Israel, a woman married a dolphin. (John-Bett)

A twenty-one-year-old North Carolina woman who "identified as blind" actually took steps to destroy her own eyesight. Others are getting doctors to paralyze them so they can live their lives in wheelchairs. They call it "transableism." (Reilly)

In Sao Paulo, Brazil, Marcelo "B-Boy" De Souza Ribeiro has chopped off two of his fingers to make his hands into a permanent V shape and peeled most of the skin off of his body so that he can look like an alien. (Hobbs)

We either understand what the will of the Lord is and act accordingly, or we must regard ourselves as worthy of being committed to an insane asylum.

A matter of power

Ephesians 5:18 *And be not drunk with wine, wherein is excess; but be filled with the Spirit;*

Here, we begin to find the power source that I wrote of earlier. If we are going to walk as the children of light in a world full of darkness, if we are going to redeem the time in these evil days, if we are going to avoid being madmen and understand what the will of the Lord is, it is going to require the filling of the Holy Spirit.

To begin with, this verse makes a very simple statement about alcohol: do not be drunk with wine. And the way he phrased it here to the Ephesians indicates that it was an action that was already happening. These dear believers, many of whom were Gentiles who had been brought into a privileged place of equality with believing Jews, were debasing themselves by becoming drunk.

And God expected it to stop.

It was not a suggestion; it was and is an absolute command.

The next phrase, "wherein is excess," is oft misunderstood. The casual reader of this often simply takes it to mean "drinking too much." But the definition of this word is "profligacy, dissolute living, debauchery." It is the same word used to describe the partying lifestyle of the prodigal son in Luke 15:13, which is there translated as "riotous." In other words, this is not simply a repetition of the first part of the verse telling people not to drink too much and get drunk. It is a warning that when we do get drunk, our lifestyle will become filthy and debased and marked by riotous partying. Drunks do not put on suits and dresses and make their way to worship with a big Bible under their hand as the sun rises; they dress to show their flesh as they make their way through the darkness to their party places.

But though all of that is true, it was not Paul's ultimate point in this verse. All of this that we have discussed is a preliminary to the ultimate point because, once Paul stated all of this, the next thing he said was, *"but be filled with the Spirit."* And once again, it was *alla*, the strong word of contrast, that he used for the word but.

So, utilizing the picture at hand, Paul was pointing out how radically a person's behavior changes when alcohol gets inside of them to such a degree that it takes control, and then he was pointing that picture to how radically a person's behavior will change when the Holy Spirit gets inside of them to such a degree that He takes control.

Every believer is indwelt by the Holy Spirit the very second that they get born again:

Romans 8:9 *But ye are not in the flesh, but in the Spirit, if so be that the Spirit of God dwell in you. Now if any man have not the Spirit of Christ, he is none of his.*

But the indwelling of the Spirit and the filling of the Spirit are two very different things.

How, then, does a person become filled with the Holy Spirit?

Qurollo correctly observed that "the believer will be controlled by the Holy Spirit by submitting his heart and mind to the Word of God." That is exactly what you see when you compare these verses to Colossians 3:16 and the verses that follow it. (108)

Holy Spirit filling is not some mystical thing that is attained by magical and uncertain means by the light of the full moon; Holy Spirit filling comes about as we bow our heart and will before the Lord's Word and allow the Holy Spirit inside of us to work that Word out in every aspect of our lives. We could put it this way: the more you stand down in your heart, the more the Holy Spirit stands up in your heart.

Another way we could put it is the same way Christ put it in the garden of Gethsemane: "Nevertheless not my will, but thine, be done."

When we get to that place, when we have so submitted our will to the will of God as expressed in His word, we will be filled with the Spirit, and therefore controlled by the Spirit, and therefore empowered by the Spirit.

A matter of praise

Ephesians 5:19 *Speaking to yourselves in psalms and hymns and spiritual songs, singing and making melody in your heart to the Lord; 20 Giving thanks always for all things unto God and the Father in the name of our Lord Jesus Christ;*

We now begin to see the plan to execute the command that I wrote of earlier. There are four categories of "ings" given from verses nineteen through twenty-one, speaking, singing and making melody, giving, and submitting. They are from four participial phrases that tie back to the filling of verse eighteen.

The first three of them that we see in verses nineteen and twenty deal with the matter of praise. We are to be speaking to ourselves in psalms and hymns and spiritual songs, we are to be singing and making melody in our hearts to the Lord, and we are to be giving thanks always for all things unto God and the Father in the name of our Lord Jesus Christ.

These things will be what flows out of a heart that is filled with the Holy Spirit. But because they are also commands found throughout Scripture, and since our filling with the Spirit is dependent on our submission to the Word, these things are unique in that they are both producers of the filling and products of the filling.

It is the loveliest of circles, really. When we submit ourselves to the Word of God by speaking to ourselves in psalms and hymns and spiritual songs, singing and making melody in our hearts to the Lord, and giving thanks, the Holy Spirit produces in us an attitude that wants to speak to ourselves in psalms and hymns and spiritual songs, sing and make melody in our hearts to the Lord, and give thanks.

As to the details of this praise, the first thing we find is that we are to be *"Speaking to yourselves* [plural] *in psalms and hymns and spiritual songs."* In other words, our conversation with other believers ought to heavily include the words of Psalms and hymns and spiritual songs. Merely speaking these words brings the power of those musical compositions to our minds and our hearts.

The second thing we find is that we are to be *"singing and making melody in your heart* [singular] *to the Lord."* Whereas the first deals with our conversation with others, this one deals with the inner soundtrack that we allow to play through our mind and heart all during the day and night.

This is legitimately a command that, in our mind, we be singing the Lord's praises in our hearts as we go about our day.

The third thing we find is that we are to be *"Giving thanks always for all things unto God and the Father in the name of our Lord Jesus Christ."*

Immediately, you know that this one is harder than the first two. How in the world are we to give thanks "always for all things"? Some things are undeniably horrific and terrible. Is this an indication that we are to be glad for the terrible and even evil things that happen in our lives?

Glad no. Grateful, yes. Those are two different things.

There is only one way that we can be thankful always for all things, and that is to remember what God does with those "all things:"

Romans 8:28 *And we know that <u>all things</u> work together for good to them that love God, to them who are the called according to his purpose.*

There will be a great many times when we cannot drag ourselves to the point of thankfulness for the details of what happens in our lives. But there should never be a point when we cannot come to the point of thankfulness for what God can and will do through all of the details of our lives.

And we are specifically to give thanks always for all things *"unto God and the Father in the name of our Lord Jesus Christ."* In other words, we give this thanks to the God who gave us our very existence which allows us to thank. And we do so in the name of our Lord Jesus Christ, who gave Himself for us and, in so doing, experienced greater agony than we will ever know so that we can experience joy that only He could know.

A matter of preference

Ephesians 5:21 *Submitting yourselves one to another in the fear of God.*

Here is the fourth "ing." The fourth thing that ties back to the filling of the Spirit in verse eighteen. And it is interesting that, before God ever got around to telling wives in this chapter to submit themselves to their husbands, He told all believers to be filled with the Spirit (which comes through submission to the Word of God) and then told all believers to submit themselves one to another.

In this verse, the simple command is to be submitting ourselves one to another in the fear of God. And again, this is both a producer of Spirit filling and a product of Spirit filling.

Both here and when used of the wife in verse twenty-two, submit is from the word *hupotasso*, and it means "to arrange under, to yield." It is a picture of giving preference to another, even over ourselves. Here is how he expressed that same concept when writing to the believers at Philippi:

Philippians 2:3 *Let nothing be done through strife or vainglory; but in lowliness of mind let each esteem other better than themselves.* **4** *Look not every man on his own things, but every man also on the things of others.*

This is how we are to behave as believers. We are to be in the habit of submitting ourselves to others rather than constantly barking orders and making demands. And we are to do all of this submitting to others "in the fear of God." In other words, He as our master and Lord has commanded this of us. We think of obeying God in terms of things like not cursing and not lying and not stealing, but we are to equally think of obeying God in terms of things like putting others before ourselves.

That is exactly what Christ did for us. So why would the Holy Spirit bother filling someone who somehow thinks that he is too good to behave toward others as Christ behaved toward him?

This matter of Spirit filling is bigger than we give it credit for. We far too often vainly go through our days as if we, in our own strength, are capable of perfectly living the Christian life. But we are no more capable of doing that than a truck is capable of pulling a load with no engine under the hood.

Do you want to bear up well as you pull the load of life each day? Then be submitted, be Spirit-filled.

Chapter Sixteen

The Model Marriage

Ephesians 5:22 *Wives, submit yourselves unto your own husbands, as unto the Lord.* **23** *For the husband is the head of the wife, even as Christ is the head of the church: and he is the saviour of the body.* **24** *Therefore as the church is subject unto Christ, so let the wives be to their own husbands in every thing.* **25** *Husbands, love your wives, even as Christ also loved the church, and gave himself for it;* **26** *That he might sanctify and cleanse it with the washing of water by the word,* **27** *That he might present it to himself a glorious church, not having spot, or wrinkle, or any such thing; but that it should be holy and without blemish.* **28** *So ought men to love their wives as their own bodies. He that loveth his wife loveth himself.* **29** *For no man ever yet hated his own flesh; but nourisheth and cherisheth it, even as the Lord the church:* **30** *For we are members of his body, of his flesh, and of his bones.* **31** *For this cause shall a man leave his father and mother, and shall be joined unto his wife, and they two shall be one flesh.* **32** *This is a great mystery: but I speak concerning Christ and the church.* **33** *Nevertheless let every one of you in particular so love his wife even as himself; and the wife see that she reverence her husband.*

    Paul has been writing at some length now to the Ephesian believers instructing them not to live as other Gentiles live. He has utilized the picture of light and darkness to remind them both of their position and their responsibility as believers. And though he has given many specifics in that regard, he is now going to get ultra-specific to one particular area of the Christian life, namely that of marriage. If there is anything in which we should not act like other Gentiles, if there is anything in which we should behave as the children of God, if there is anything in which we should actually be the light in this world, it is in our marriages.

A submission required

Ephesians 5:22 *Wives, submit yourselves unto your own husbands, as unto the Lord.* **23** *For the husband is the head of the wife, even as Christ is the head of the church: and he is the saviour of the body.* **24** *Therefore as the church is subject unto Christ, so let the wives be to their own husbands in every thing.*

If Paul had sat down to write and said, "I am going to do my very best to write something that worldly women 2,000 years from now will hate with a passion," he could not have done any better of a job than he did under the inspiration of the Holy Ghost in these verses. In fact, if he had merely said, "I am going to do my very best to write something that weak and carnal men 2,000 years from now will hate with a passion," he still could not have done any better of a job than he did under the inspiration of the Holy Ghost in these verses.

If you produced a magic pen with which you could strike one passage of Scripture from the Bible and have it disappear from every Bible on earth, every feminist on earth would snatch that pen and head straight for this passage, and every effeminate man on earth would snatch that pen and head straight for this passage.

And yet, love it or hate it, this passage is every bit as scriptural and authoritative as John 3:16.

Paul begins with the command, *"Wives, submit yourselves unto your own husbands, as unto the Lord."* Submit is from the word *hupattaso,* and it means "to arrange yourself under the authority of another, to submit, to obey, to yield to." Clearly, that is not something that anyone's flesh enjoys, whether it be to God or to government or to spouse or to parents. But it is nonetheless a command; the wife is to submit herself to her own husband as unto the Lord.

There are some things of note that should be said here. To begin with, there is no command or even any inference that the man is to "keep his wife in line/in subjection." No, this command is entirely to the ladies. Any man who arrives at the unbiblical conclusion that he is to "keep his wife in line" *is* biblically illiterate and *will be* in for a very rude awakening in life. This is not an ogre verse; this is a princess verse. This command is to daughters of the King, from the King.

Secondly, there is no command or even any inference that women are to be in subjection to all other men. In fact, the text very specifically says the words *"your own husbands."* You may be blissfully unaware of this, but there is a pretty wide stupid streak running through a few Christian circles where men actually believe that any woman is to be subject to all of the men in the room, whatever the room is, and whoever the men are. I read one of the social media posts from one of these clowns very recently, and he legitimately and specifically argued that all women are to be subject to all men, no matter who those men are.

It is almost hard to quantify that level of stupidity.

Paul meant what he said here, *"Wives, submit yourselves unto your own husbands."*

Some years ago, one of these idiots sashayed his quarter-ton self into Dana's office, slapped a stack of papers on her desk, and barked, "Make copies of these for me."

She slapped the papers right back at him and barked back, "Do it yourself!"

Good for her; she wasn't married to Bluto; she was and is married to me.

A church not too very far from mine hired a youth pastor. Not too long after, they put together a youth trip. On the day in question, the kids were piling into a couple of vans for the trip. The pastor's wife was coming along as a chaperone, and she knew all of the kids far better than this wet behind the ears Bible college graduate. She saw some very clear problems brewing in some of the seating arrangements and suggested that they quickly change a few things. To which the youth pastor responded by sticking his finger in her face and saying, "Stay in your place, woman; I'll handle this."

If that had been my wife, he had done that to, I would have beaten the dirt out of him before I fired him.

The very picture painted in this passage clearly necessitates a wife being in submission to exactly one man, her own husband. And, based on the picture of marriage as being a representation of Christ and the church as we see in this passage, if a woman is to be submissive to every man, not just her own husband, then the church must also be submissive to Muhammad and Joseph Smith and Charles Taze Russell and Confucius.

But all of that said, the wife absolutely is to submit to her own husband. She is to voluntarily and willingly come under his authority. But do you know the real beauty of this? If a man behaves himself as he should, this will *normally* not be an issue. I have been married to Dana for nearly thirty years now, and I have focused all of my energy in marriage to loving her as Christ has loved the church. And because of that, I have not had one ounce of pushback from her on this issue of leadership and submission. She allows me to lead because I love her like Christ loves the church.

Not all wives do, though, and Paul's words come as a stinging rebuke to those who do not, those who defy the "normally" paradigm I wrote of a moment ago. We had a couple in our church many years ago, and the husband, to be blunt, was warned and yet made a really dumb decision anyway in the woman that he married. Of all people, the girl's own father told the young man, "Boy, just be aware, nobody can tell that girl anything." And yet, he married her anyway, and she has defied this command of Scripture every single day of their marriage for decades now. She even openly brags about it online. She runs that home; she knows it, he knows it, and everyone else knows it. And if by chance she is saved, which I highly doubt, but if by some chance she is, she will answer to God for her wicked disobedience just as much as a drunkard or fornicator will. The wife is to submit herself to her own husband "*as unto the Lord,*" meaning "just as she would submit to the Lord Himself."

Ephesians 5:23 *For the husband is the head of the wife, even as Christ is the head of the church: and he is the saviour of the body.*

Verse twenty-three gives us the why of the command of verse twenty-two. The wife is to submit herself unto her husband for (because) the husband is the head of the wife. There is no real need to encourage a man to be the head of his wife, his home; he already is the head of his home. There is only a need to encourage a man to act as the head of his home since he already is the head anyway. And the man is the head of the wife/home even as, just as, Christ is the head of the church and the Savior of the body.

There is no question that Christ is the head of the church. There is equally no question that the man is the head of the wife/home.

But there is an essential addendum added, *"and he is the saviour of the body."* You cannot separate those two things; just as Christ laid down His life for the church and therefore has the right to lead it, the man is to lay down his life for the wife and home if he expects to have the right to lead it. Sir, you do not get the sovereignty without the sacrifice. If you expect the wife to play the role of the submissive church, then you have to play the role of the sacrificed Christ.

I know that many men would love to separate these two things. Many men would love for this to be based on chromosomes rather than on Calvary. But that simply is not the case. The church willingly submits to Christ because Christ laid down His life for the church. The wife willingly submits to the husband when the husband lays down his life for the home. In other words, if you, Sir, are serving yourself and promoting yourself and pampering yourself, you have no legitimate right to expect the wife to behave to you like the church behaves to Christ.

But on the other side of the coin, any woman who chooses feminism over submission is also unbiblical and out of order. There are no perfect men, but there are a great number of very good men who nonetheless have wives who view submission as if it were a four-letter word. It is not, and the husband is still head of the wife whether anyone likes it or not.

Ephesians 5:24 *Therefore as the church is subject unto Christ, so let the wives be to their own husbands in every thing.*

The phrase at the end of this verse is going to be very problematic if you neglect the "therefore" at the beginning of the verse. In other words, if you take the command "*let the wives be subject to their own husbands in everything*" out of the context provided by the "therefore," you are going to come up with a paradigm in which the husband becomes more authoritative than God Himself, even when he commands wickedness of the wife. Here, then, is what the therefore refers back to:

Ephesians 5:23 *For the husband is the head of the wife, even as Christ is the head of the church: and he is the saviour of the body.*

The phrase at the end of verse twenty-four goes right back to the husband behaving in a Christlike and sacrificial manner to the wife as Christ did to the church. And here is why that is such an important distinction to observe: the church can always be subject to Christ safely without fear of Him commanding anything sinful or wicked of us. The wife is supposed to always be able to be subject to her husband safely without fear of him commanding anything sinful or wicked of her.

But you and I both know that is not always the case.

Driving down the road some years ago, I had the radio on to try to keep me awake late at night as I drove home. I was scanning the stations, trying to find something decent, and I heard a lady's voice talking. It caught my attention, so I listened for a moment. As it turns out, it was a rather prominent lady radio Bible teacher. She was reading a letter from another woman who had written in asking her a question. The lady's husband was a nonbeliever and a very wicked and perverted man. This lady wrote, "I am a Christian, and I know that I am commanded to set no wicked thing before my eyes, Psalm 101:3. But my husband wants me to go with him to the 'adult bookstore' and go into their little theater and watch pornographic movies with him. What should I do?"

The lady Bible teacher quoted **Ephesians 5:24,** *"Therefore as the church is subject unto Christ, so let the wives be to their own husbands in every thing,"* and said, "Oh, dear one, you may not like going to that movie, but be subject to your husband in everything. Maybe the Lord will have him fall asleep so that you can close your eyes and will not have to watch."

In addition to being plainly stupid, it is also the most devilish twisting and mangling of this verse I can possibly imagine. When you take this verse out of the context of the husband behaving in a sacrificial and Christlike manner toward the wife, when you make it universally applicable to all men in all situations no matter their behavior, then you have very literally subordinated the will of God to the will of wicked men!

A lady began to visit our church without her husband, and she was very "proper" in the way she dressed and talked and acted. She carried a huge Bible under her arm and looked much like Laura Ingles in appearance. But within a two-week period of time, she took great umbrage both at what I preached in regard to this very text and in what was said in a ladies' Sunday School class that matched my teaching. And when I say that she took great umbrage, I mean that she, a visitor, loudly and openly proclaimed me and my teacher and our church to be wrong in our view. She said, "A wife is to obey her husband no matter what he asks, period."

Our ladies were shocked; I was suspicious. So I did some digging...

As it turns out, her husband "liked" children. As in, he was a registered sexual predator, a pedophile. And multiple pastors that I contacted warned me that he would send his wife to churches to gain an open door and then eventually invite the children from those churches over to their house for "fun activities."

So, should she really have been obeying his commands to her in this? Should she honestly have been helping to provide him with children to molest?

Peter said something that is very applicable to this argument:

Acts 5:29 *Then Peter and the other apostles answered and said, We ought to obey God rather than men.*

This should be your governing principle in all matters of wickedness.

Should a wife be looking for excuses to disobey her husband? Certainly not; if she is, she is unsubmissive and rebellious and not the least bit pleasing in the sight of God. And there will be times, even in Christian homes, where the wife must submit to her husband "in everything" even when he is wrong – as long as he is not demanding disobedience to God.

We had a couple in our church many years ago, and the husband was a very good and godly man but a few French fries short of a Happy Meal on practical matters. Gasoline has always been a bit cheaper in South Carolina. So he demanded that his wife drive the vehicle all the way to South Carolina from their house a couple of times a week to fill it up with gas. So, she did some math. She put down on paper what the gas mileage of their vehicle was, how far they were from the nearest station in South Carolina, and how much they would save per gallon versus how much they would waste in gasoline going to get it and coming home.

They would have come out far better simply buying gasoline at the station just down the road from their house. And yet, he could not wrap his mind around that; math was not his strong suit, to put it mildly. So he just brushed it off and told her to keep getting it in South Carolina.

Pay very careful attention: he was not asking her to do anything sinful. And he was a good man who was sacrificing himself for her good and the good of the home. So, very dutifully and without complaint, she drove to South Carolina a couple of times a week to get gas, knowing good and well it was actually costing them money to do so.

Good for her. That is exactly the right heart attitude on this subject.

A standard revealed

Ephesians 5:25 *Husbands, love your wives, even as Christ also loved the church, and gave himself for it;* **26** *That he might sanctify and cleanse it with the washing of water by the word,* **27** *That he might present it to himself a glorious church, not having spot, or wrinkle, or any such thing; but that it should be holy and without blemish.* **28** *So ought men to love their wives as their own bodies. He that loveth his wife loveth himself.* **29** *For no man ever yet hated his own flesh; but nourisheth and* *cherisheth it, even as the Lord the church:* **30** *For we are members of his body, of his flesh, and of his bones.*

After the fall, in the garden of Eden, God said a very few short words to Eve – and then gave a monologue to Adam. And here, in Ephesians, God once again said a very few short words to the woman – and now gives a monologue to the man. Many men would have you believe that Ephesians 5 contains exactly one verse, namely verse twenty-two. It does not. God said a short few words to the woman and then turned and really piled the bulk of the responsibility for how things go in the home on the man.

The first thing He said was one long sentence spread across three verses:

Ephesians 5:25 *Husbands, love your wives, even as Christ also loved the church, and gave himself for it;* **26** *That he might sanctify and cleanse it with the washing of water by the word,* **27** *That he might present it to himself a glorious church, not having spot, or wrinkle, or any such thing; but that it should be holy and without blemish.*

Many husbands enjoy verse twenty-two without really thinking about it. Those same husbands enjoy not thinking about verses twenty-five through twenty-seven.

Husbands are to love their wives "even as" Christ loved the church. As is so often the case, that phrase "even as" comes from the word *kathos,* meaning according to, in like manner as, and to the same degree as. Men are to love their wives according to the way Christ loved the church, in the same manner as Christ loved the church, and to the same degree as Christ loved the church and gave Himself for it. Christ left the high estate of heaven to come to the low estate of earth for the church. Christ put up with the hot-headedness and dimwittedness of the twelve men with which He started the church. Christ washed the nasty feet of the church. Christ forgave the church when "the church" denied Him three times and even cursed in so doing. Christ literally died for the church. And through it all, not one time was He ever less than absolutely loving to the church.

And the same Bible and the same chapter that commands the wife to be subject to the husband commands the man to love his wife like this. If a man will simply not be a jerk, if he will truly love his wife, a truly godly wife will never, ever have any trouble submitting to him!

When I was in Bible college, one of my advisors was a really godly black gentleman. And I mention his race simply because one day, I actually got to see him turn white! He was walking through the hall, and he was so angry that he was visibly shaking, and the color had drained from his face; I am telling you that he was so mad he actually looked like he was turning white. I called him by name and said, "What is wrong with you?"

He replied, "I just found out that some of our male married students have been 'disciplining their wives' to put them in subjection. Some of them have been physically spanking them like children; others have been grounding them by telling them that they cannot make eye contact with or speak to anyone else on the campus."

I started laughing. I mean, I really lost it.

He looked at me like I had lost my mind and said, "Why are you laughing, Wagner?"

I replied, "Because I am imagining how hilarious it would be if any of them tried something like that with a woman like my wife!"

As the sentence goes on, Paul explains the why behind Christ loving the church like He did and does:

Ephesians 5:26 *That he might sanctify and cleanse it with the washing of water by the word,* **27** *That he might present it to himself a glorious church, not having spot, or wrinkle, or any such thing; but that it should be holy and without blemish.*

Christ first of all loved the church like He loved it so that He could sanctify it. Sanctified is from the word *hagiadzo,* and it means "to separate from others and consecrate to oneself." In other words, Christ loved the church like He loved it so that the church would become completely separate from all other suitors and completely joined to Him in its affection.

Let that sink in as it applies to marriage.

Sir, your job is to love your wife so well that in her affections, she completely separates from all other suitors and wholly joins to you. If I could really simplify that, you are to love her so well that she never wants anybody else.

The second reason he gives for how Christ loved the church is that He might *"cleanse it with the washing of water by the word."*

In the ancient world, before a wedding, a woman would often spend weeks or even months cleansing and anointing herself in anticipation of the wedding night. Here is a pretty famous example of that:

Esther 2:12 *Now when every maid's turn was come to go in to king Ahasuerus, after that she had been twelve months, according to the manner of the women, (for so were the days of their purifications accomplished, to wit, six months with oil of myrrh, and six months with sweet odours, and with other things for the purifying of the women;)*

Twelve months! Six months being treated with myrrh oil, six months having sweet odors applied, and the entire time "other things" for purifying. Mind you, this custom (despite Ahasuerus' obvious perverting of it) was not to make the woman into the wife; it was to prepare the one who had already been chosen as the wife to enter into intimacy with her husband.

But in the case of Christ and His bride, it is not myrrh or spices with which He anoints us; it is the washing of water by the Word. This is talking about the Scripture and how it prepares us for intimacy with Christ. Christ did not just give Himself for us so that we could escape hell; He gave Himself for us so that we can be clean and presentable in His sight as well.

Husbands, do not forget that this picture is being applied to marriage. In other words, if you really love your wife, you will be working to present her spotless to yourself rather than working to present her to a leering world. Once again, think of the example found in the book of Esther. Ahasuerus, that wretched and scummy example of a husband, tried to present his wife, Vashti, to his leering and drunken buddies. That kind of thing is the exact opposite of the picture presented here. It is beyond bewildering to see husbands in our day intentionally trying to draw inappropriate attention to their wives. And there is a generation of social influencers that is teaching this filthiness to boys. A rather famous one, a "conservative influencer" who used to be an MMA fighter, boasts about turning his girlfriends into porn stars.

You should have nothing but loathing for a perverted little creep like that.

Husbands, all of your words and actions are to be designed to make your wife a clean person, not a dirty person, a person for one man, you, not for all others. Verse twenty-seven summarizes all of that really well:

Ephesians 5:27 *That he might present it to himself a glorious church, not having spot, or wrinkle, or any such thing; but that it should be holy and without blemish.*

We see once again that Christ is not just interested in rescuing us from the fire; He is interested in making us glorious. Jesus did everything that He did on Calvary so that we could be "a glorious church," a church that does not have a spot or wrinkle or any such thing, any defect in His sight. But, strong contrast, we are to be holy and without blemish.

Do you see from these words how Christ views sinfulness in us? He views it as an ugly and unattractive thing. He views it as a blemish. And we should as well. Anything sinful in us should look really unattractive to us. People will spend hours in front of the mirror trying to make themselves look good physically; how much more should we spend time in front of the mirror of God's Word trying to make ourselves look good to the One who loved us enough to die for us?

But again, remember that Paul is also applying all of this to the husband's responsibility in marriage. The husband is to help his wife be a holy and righteous and godly daughter of the king. Anything that you do, Sir, to lead your wife into sin or to hinder her from righteousness is wicked and abominable in the sight of God.

It is so ugly for a man to try and keep his wife out of church. It is so ugly for a man to try to keep his wife from her Bible. It is so ugly for a man to try to get his wife to drink or to do drugs. It is so ugly for a man to try and get his wife to be immodest online so that he can look good to all of his weird buddies. Anything that you do to lead your wife into sin or to hinder her from righteousness is wicked and abominable in the sight of God.

Ephesians 5:28 *So ought men to love their wives as their own bodies. He that loveth his wife loveth himself.*

I have often humorously observed of a particular man that if he loved his wife half as much as he loved himself, she would feel like the most loved woman on earth. He really does adore himself; every mirror is his favorite thing, and every luxury desired of his heart becomes a reality in his life.

But this verse teaches a truth far beyond that "half as much" standard. Every husband is to love his wife as if she were his own body. And, as motivation toward that end, Paul closes the sentence by saying, *"He that loveth his wife loveth himself."* If that sounds a bit like the modern maxim, "Happy wife, happy life," please understand that it is supposed to. This verse is genuinely teaching that if you truly love yourself, you will love your wife because it is to your benefit to do so!

Those who treat their wives like treasure rather than trash generally find themselves treated like lovers rather than losers.

Ephesians 5:29 *For no man ever yet hated his own flesh; but nourisheth and cherisheth it, even as the Lord the church:* **30** *For we are members of his body, of his flesh, and of his bones.*

What are we to do with verse twenty-nine in light of the many people who get professional counseling for their self-loathing, or drink to forget who and what they are, or even take their own lives? We are simply to recognize it as true. You see, all of those things are actually proofs of the truth of this verse, not evidence against it! If a man did not love himself, he would feel no need for counseling or for drinking to forget or for taking his own life to make the pain go away. Every man does indeed love his own flesh.

People nourish and cherish their flesh; in other words, they see to their own comfort and well-being. And they do so *"even as the Lord the church!"* People sacrifice for themselves and are faithful to themselves. And Paul uses that as an example of how the husbands are to treat their wives. You are to treat her in the exact way that you would treat yourself in her position. You are to care for her as if she is you. And the next verse gives an interesting motivation to that:

Ephesians 5:30 *For we are members of his body, of his flesh, and of his bones.*

The Lord nourishes and cherishes the church because we are members of His body, of His flesh, and of His bones. He has brought us into oneness and unity with Himself. The man, when he marries, does the same thing for the wife, and that will be examined more fully in the next verse. For now, just understand that Christ expects us to treat our wives like He treats the church and like we treat our own bodies. And since we humans are flawed at best, even in our love for ourselves, a man's ultimate standard for how he interacts with his wife ought to be how Christ interacted with the church, and we should never settle for anything less.

A singular re-creation

Ephesians 5:31 *For this cause shall a man leave his father and mother, and shall be joined unto his wife, and they two shall be one flesh.*

This is a bit tricky, but when Paul starts this verse with the words "for this cause," he is not referring back to a cause that came before it in the text; he is actually quoting another verse entirely.

Genesis 2:24 *Therefore shall a man leave his father and his mother, and shall cleave unto his wife: and they shall be one flesh.*

Therefore and for this cause are the same thing. What Paul has done, in the midst of a message about marriage, is insert another verse from Scripture, just like a preacher would do today, giving a foundation for his words to stand on. Both Paul here and Moses as he wrote that text in Genesis, were pointing out that there will only ever be one "one flesh union" on earth, that of a man and wife. They were both alluding to the fact that since Adam had originally just been one person, and then God came by and took flesh and blood and bone out of Adam to make Eve, when those two come back together, they are re-creating the one flesh that they used to be.

And while there was only one original Adam and Eve, the same thing still holds true for every marriage. The man and the woman come together as one flesh; they become one unit, one body, as it were. Rightly viewed, there is no stronger bond on earth than this. And when a man and woman view it in this light, they do not take marriage lightly in the least.

Our day is beset by divorce in epidemic proportions because men and women view themselves as individuals in a marriage there to please themselves rather than as one flesh, never to be parted, with each side of the equation seeking only the highest good of the other.

A supernatural revelation

Ephesians 5:32 *This is a great mystery: but I speak concerning Christ and the church.*

As we have observed so often, a mystery in New Testament terms was something that was true from the oldest of times but was just now being revealed. From the very beginning of time, God designed the man and woman relationship with Himself and the church in mind. From the very beginning of time, He designed marriage to be a picture of His love for the church and how He and the church would operate in that relationship. This was not an afterthought; it was not something that the church dreamed up in the fourth century, it was the plan of God before there ever was an Adam and an Eve and this thing called marriage.

A simple regulation

Ephesians 5:33 *Nevertheless let every one of you in particular so love his wife even as himself; and the wife see that she reverence her husband.*

Paul took his readers to the heights of the heavens with the revelation of the mystery that God designed human marriage as a picture of His love for and relationship with the church. But now, as the chapter ends, he gives a "nevertheless" that brings it all back down to ground level.

Paul refers to *"every one of you in particular."* That is a unique old English way of saying, "each and every one of you as individuals." So, from the high and lofty subject of Christ loving the church and picturing that utilizing the marriage of man and woman, he turns to each and every single individual and says, in so many words, "But let's get really practical here; the main thing you need to focus on is that you husbands need to truly love your wives and you wives need to truly reverence, venerate, your husbands."

You see, theological concepts are much easier for us to deal with than practical responsibilities. Anyone can spend hours examining the theological ramifications of Christ's union with the church; far fewer husbands are willing to wash the dishes for their weary wives, and far fewer wives are willing to say, "Yes sir," to their husbands. But the model marriage is not a theological construct; it is theology in work clothes. It is us living in the privacy of our homes in such a way as to make God in heaven say, "Hey, look at that! That looks just like me and the church!"

Chapter Seventeen
Obedience and Gentleness

Ephesians 6:1 *Children, obey your parents in the Lord: for this is right.* **2** *Honour thy father and mother; (which is the first commandment with promise;)* **3** *That it may be well with thee, and thou mayest live long on the earth.* **4** *And, ye fathers, provoke not your children to wrath: but bring them up in the nurture and admonition of the Lord.* **5** *Servants, be obedient to them that are your masters according to the flesh, with fear and trembling, in singleness of your heart, as unto Christ;* **6** *Not with eyeservice, as menpleasers; but as the servants of Christ, doing the will of God from the heart;* **7** *With good will doing service, as to the Lord, and not to men:* **8** *Knowing that whatsoever good thing any man doeth, the same shall he receive of the Lord, whether he be bond or free.* **9** *And, ye masters, do the same things unto them, forbearing threatening: knowing that your Master also is in heaven; neither is there respect of persons with him.*

Paul's most famous words for the family are behind us. But he is not yet quite finished with that subject. You see, there is often more than just a husband and wife in the family. And for that matter, there are other human relationships to consider as we strive to not "be like other Gentiles."

Expectations for children

Ephesians 6:1 *Children, obey your parents in the Lord: for this is right.* **2** *Honour thy father and mother; (which is the* *first commandment with promise;)* **3** *That it may be well with thee, and thou mayest live long on the earth.*

In the last chapter, I observed that if there is anything in which we should not act like other Gentiles, if there is anything in which we should behave as the children of God, if there is anything in which we should actually be the light in this world, it is in our marriages. But now let me observe that, as a close second, if there is anything in which we should behave as the children of God, if there is anything in which we should actually be the light in this world, it is in our parent/child relationships. And Paul begins to examine that truth in these verses as he gives some divine expectations for children.

He begins with the simple words, *"Children, obey your parents."* In our day, the day in which the more common paradigm is for parents to obey their children, these words come as a shock to the culture. Nonetheless, they still stand true, and God has not changed His expectations on the subject. Children are to obey their parents, not the other way around.

On a practical level, this makes perfect sense. Parents have been around far longer, they know far more, and they are more capable of discerning a good idea from a bad one and the proper way of doing things. But even aside from the practical nature of this command, children should still obey their parents simply because this is the nature of the structure that God Himself has put in place. Any parent obeying their children is out of order, and any children not obeying their parents are out of order.

In the church of my younger years, there were two families in the same congregation yet on different paths. Family number one, we will call them the Jones, was a very "modern and enlightened" sort of family. They had two children, and the children called the shots in the home in clothing, entertainment, activities, morality, pretty much everything. The parents were there merely to accommodate the desires of their children. Family number two, we will call them the Smiths, was very different. The Smiths had three children, all of which were expected to obey their parents. And while the Jones family never butted heads because the children always got what they wanted, the Smith family had a lot of headbutting, a lot of tense moments, because the mother and father quite regularly told their children "No."

The "smooth sailing" of the Jones family, though, turned into a sinking ship as the children got older; the young adult children continued the process of feeding their flesh until it destroyed them and their parents. Mom and Dad tried to stop it once they saw the direction everything was heading, but it was too late. Years of long-established acquiescence could not be undone in a day. The head butting of the Smith family, though, turned into a heavenly beauty as the children got older; the young adult children continued the process of doing what was right, and God blessed them and their parents. Mom and Dad continued to encourage everything, seeing the direction it was headed, and they were successful. Years of long-established righteousness produced blessings for a lifetime.

Children, obey your parents, and parents, expect your children to obey.

This is to be done "in the Lord," as the next phrase spells out clearly.

Jamieson, Fausset and Brown said of this, "Both parents and children being Christians 'in the Lord,' expresses the element in which the obedience is to take place, and the motive to obedience." (419)

Albert Barnes put it this way, "In the Lord. That is, as far as their commandments agree with those of God, and no farther. No parent can have a right to require a child to steal, or lie, or cheat, or assist him in committing murder, or in doing any other wrong thing. No parent has a right to forbid a child to pray, to read the Bible, to worship God, or to make a profession of religion. The duties and rights of children, in such cases, are similar to those of wives." (Linder)

Those are accurate views of the text. In other words, parents, just as with the rule of the husband and submission of the wife, you have no right to expect the obedience afforded to the Lord when you act like the devil. That said, children, even the children of godly parents, are bent toward rebellion; it is in our fallen nature. This text and command serve as a warning siren to kids who have godly parents that they refuse to obey. If you disobey godly parents giving godly commands, then you are disobeying God Himself because His command in this passage is for you to obey your parents in the Lord.

If a mother or father sees a child beginning to show interest in a boy or girl that they should not be with, it should be as simple as those parents saying, "No," and the child saying, "I will obey your wishes."

If a mother or father sees a child beginning to hang around a wrong crowd, it should be as simple as those parents saying, "Don't get around them anymore," and the child saying, "I won't."

Children are to obey their parents in the Lord.

The last phrase of verse one says, *"for this is right."* Simply put, it is wrong to disobey and right to obey. If you disobey your parents, you are doing wrong.

Ephesians 6:2 *Honour thy father and mother; (which is the first commandment with promise;)* **3** *That it may be well with thee, and thou mayest live long on the earth.*

These two verses contain both a quote and a commentary. This passage is a restatement of the fifth commandment as found in the following passages:

Exodus 20:12 *Honour thy father and thy mother: that thy days may be long upon the land which the LORD thy God giveth thee.*

Deuteronomy 5:16 *Honour thy father and thy mother, as the LORD thy God hath commanded thee; that thy days may be prolonged, and that it may go well with thee, in the land which the LORD thy God giveth thee.*

The commentary is found in the parenthesis of verse two, *"which is the first commandment with promise."* The first four commandments contained no specific, targeted promise for the individual who obeys. This one did and does. God promised that a child who honors mother and father would live a long life and a blessed life. Mind you, he is speaking in comparative terms; not every child who honors mom and dad lives to be ninety, or even seventy, nor does everyone live an easy life. But every child who honors mom and dad lives longer than they would have had they dishonored them, and every child who honors his or her parents will be more blessed of God than had they not.

God is very serious about this matter of children honoring their parents. Honor is from the word *timao*, and it means "to assign an exceedingly high value to something or someone and to act accordingly." Children who berate or belittle their parents, children who disrespect them, will have the omniscient God of heaven marking days off of their lives and blessings as well.

Expectations for fathers

Ephesians 6:4 *And, ye fathers, provoke not your children to wrath: but bring them up in the nurture and admonition of the Lord.*

The first phrase of verse four is one that often leaves people utterly perplexed. What exactly did Paul mean when he told the fathers not to provoke their children to wrath? After all, children get angry pretty easily, even when they are told things like, "Don't stick that key in the light socket!" So, are we as parents to avoid doing anything that might make our precious little Bubbas and Lulus angry? Are we to allow them to take the entire box of frozen popsicles to bed with them just so they will not be upset at us taking them away?

The phrase *provoke not your children to wrath* means, "Do not exasperate them to the point of anger and resentfulness." But that still does not really help us, does it? Children get exasperated to the point of anger and resentfulness over a great deal of things, even things like not being allowed to stay up all night playing video games instead of going to sleep and getting ready for school the next day.

Fortunately, this verse defines the term for us by contrast. The entire verse says, *"And, ye fathers, provoke not your children to wrath: but* [alla, strong contrast] *bring them up in the nurture and admonition of the Lord.* So, whatever *provoke not your children to wrath* is, it is the opposite of *bring them up in the nurture and admonition of the Lord.*

Bring them up is from the word *ektrephete*, and it means "to feed and to raise." Nurture is from *paideia*, and it means "to instruct and to train." Admonition is from the word *nouthesia,* and it means "to instruct, to exhort, to build up." So fathers are to spiritually feed and raise their children by instructing and training and exhorting and building them up in the Lord. And that tells us that "provoking our children to wrath" is the opposite; it is the father who insults rather than instructs, terrifies rather than trains, excoriates rather than exhorts, and belittles rather than builds up. In summary, it is the picture of a father who expects his children to behave as and appear as good little drones so that he can look good to others and seeks to accomplish that by using misery as motivation.

He had a wife and five children. He was "called to preach" and brought his family to Bible college with him. And he also openly disdained all of the horrible "hicks and rubes" in churches all around us who "did not know how to raise their children for God." His children dressed perfectly and acted perfectly and never got dirty and were never allowed to interact with other kids. They also never smiled, that I saw. Any sign of "normalcy" in his children was immediately and sternly corrected. I never heard him laugh or cut up with them, I never saw him play with them, I never heard him teach them anything, it was all demands all day every day, and they never could quite measure up. And one by one by one, as soon as they got old enough to bolt, every last one of them did.

Every. One.

And every single one of them detests God and church and Christians to this day.

That man directly disobeyed the command of this verse, and he will answer to God for destroying his children in so doing.

Fathers, yes, you must uphold the Biblical standards of right and wrong in your home. But you must also be your children's biggest cheerleader and fiercest advocate and greatest comfort and most consistent teacher.

Of all of the gifts my children have given me, one of the ones that I value the very most is a simple card that my youngest daughter wrote to me.

It says:

"Hey dad, thank you so much for everything. You work so incredibly hard to provide for our family. You love people so well, and you are always there for us.

You are dedicated to the ministry that you have been called to, and you are the most amazing example of what it means to be faithful. Thank you for raising me in a Christian home and for teaching me about God. Thank you for being patient and kind, you're always there to hold me when I cry, then tell me some stupid joke to make me laugh. I wouldn't want to find out that I have neuropathy from anyone else. The thing that I love most about you is that you love God more than you love me or anyone else. I know I can follow you because you are following Christ (1 Cor. 11:1). I thank God for giving me you as a dad, and I hope you know that I see Jesus in you.

I love you, Dad."

I framed it, and it is sitting on my desk at the house.

Fathers, we have a responsibility to foster this type of relationship with our children; we have a responsibility to bring them up in the nurture and admonition of the Lord.

Expectations for servants

Ephesians 6:5 *Servants, be obedient to them that are your masters according to the flesh, with fear and trembling, in singleness of your heart, as unto Christ;* **6** *Not with eyeservice, as menpleasers; but as the servants of Christ, doing the will of God from the heart;* **7** *With good will doing service, as to the Lord, and not to men:* **8** *Knowing that whatsoever good thing any man doeth, the same shall he receive of the Lord, whether he be bond or free.*

To say that this passage brings up a touchy topic would be an understatement. And yet, it need not be ignored, first of all because it is in the Bible, and secondly because its scope is actually wider than most people imagine.

Adam Clarke said of this passage:

"Though *doulon* frequently signifies a slave or bondman, yet it often implies a servant in general, or any one bound to another, either for a limited time, or for life. Even a slave, if a Christian, was bound to serve him faithfully by whose money he was bought, howsoever illegal that traffic may be considered. In heathen countries slavery was in some sort excusable; among Christians it is an enormity and a crime for which perdition has scarcely an adequate state of punishment." (6:467)

That is pretty well said. In a nutshell, hell itself could never be hot enough for any Christians participating in slavery. Heathen nations may not know better, but nations with access to the Word of God should and should have, including our own. But right or wrong, Paul did not justify slavery; he simply looked at an established institution and gave instructions from God even for that. And one reason for that is that, in the ancient world, slavery was generally radically different from what we saw and see in the modern world. A study of the Old Testament laws on the subject show that comparing their slavery to modern slavery is not like comparing apples to oranges; it is more akin to comparing apples to carburetors.

But with all of that said, slavery was still very real in Paul's day, and many people he wrote to would have been bondslaves. And in those days, rather than a situation in which someone was sold by their own people into the bondage of another, the bondslave was normally one who had gotten himself into debt and could not get out, and so he indentured himself to another for a specified period of time in order to pay his debts.

And Paul's instruction to people in that state was, *"Servants, be obedient to them that are your masters according to the flesh, with fear and trembling, in singleness of your heart, as unto Christ."*

Servants were to obey their masters as children were to obey their parents and wives were to obey their husbands. And they were to do so with fear and trembling; there were consequences for disobedience. They were also to do so in singleness of heart, as unto Christ, and that means "Not merely through fear of punishment, but from a principle of uprightness, serving them as you would serve Christ." (6:467)

In other words, they were to obey not just to have their debts paid and not just to avoid punishment but because it was right to do so, just as it was right to serve Christ.

But remember that, as Clarke observed, the term *doulon* also applied to more than just a slave; it also applied to servants in general, or as we would put it, employees. So, while slavery was wonderfully obliterated in the Western world more than a century ago, the principles found in these verses still apply beautifully to the employer/employee paradigm still found in our world today.

If someone is writing us a paycheck, it is right for us to obey them while we are on the clock unless they are commanding us to disobey the Lord. "Move that box of widgets," yes. "Lie on that bill of lading," no. And slaves and servants then and employees now are to do so *"Not with eyeservice, as menpleasers; but as the servants of Christ, doing the will of God from the heart; With good will doing service, as to the Lord, and not to men: Knowing that whatsoever good thing any man doeth, the same shall he receive of the Lord, whether he be bond or free."*

"Not with eyeservice, as menpleasers," means not like people who just put on a good performance to make people happy. The phrase that follows, *"but as the servants of Christ, doing the will of God from the heart,"* gives us that same truth from the contrasting perspective, teaching us that we are to work and obey as the servants of Christ, doing the will of God from the heart, not just trying to please men's eyes. No one should ever be a better, more conscientious, more dependable employee than a child of God.

Further expounding on this truth, Paul said, *"With good will doing service, as to the Lord, and not to men."* This means "Doing your job with kindness and benevolence as if you were working for the Lord rather than men."

This goes far beyond obedience; it goes all the way down to attitude.

The final instruction Paul gave to servants was a bit of encouragement, *"Knowing that whatsoever good thing any man doeth, the same shall he receive of the Lord, whether he be bond or free."*

The servants of his day may never have received the blessings and accolades from their master that they were due; but they would absolutely receive those blessings and accolades from the Lord, whether they were serving as a bondman or a free man. When we do right, God will bless us no matter our station in life.

Expectations for masters

Ephesians 6:9 *And, ye masters, do the same things unto them, forbearing threatening: knowing that your Master also is in heaven; neither is there respect of persons with him.*

I need you to understand how unbelievably radical this verse was in the ancient world. When Paul wrote these words, very few people if any at all were saying anything like them. Paul told the Masters to *"do the same things unto them,"* meaning to their servants. Those "same things" refer back to the kindness and respect that he demanded of the servants of the master in the previous verses.

Let that sink in.

It was not very shocking at all to hear someone say to servants, "Be very kind and respectful to your masters." but it was pretty much unheard of to hear someone say to masters, "Be just as kind and respectful to your servants as you expect them to be to you." But that is exactly what Paul said. And while the Jews would not be surprised at that based on what the law of Moses had to say of servitude, the heathen world would be stunned by it; they knew nothing of that sort of a master. Masters routinely used threats and threatening. But here was Paul giving them the most unheard-of command: forebear threatening. That means to send it back, to give it up.

Send threatening back to the pit from whence it came; give it up forever.

On what basis would he give such instructions? The answer is twofold. One, *"knowing that your Master also is in heaven."* In other words, every master had a master. And those human masters had God in heaven as their Master, the God who sees everything and knows everything and will not tolerate ill behavior on the part of His servants toward their servants. Two, *"neither is there respect of persons with him."* By this, masters were to understand that they were no better in God's sight than the servants they were over. God was not going to give them a pass on bad behavior toward their servants because they were the masters; everyone is under God, and He expects good behavior from His creation toward His creation.

And once again, all of this applies beautifully even today in the employer/employee paradigm. Every employer ought to treat their employees with dignity and respect, understanding that they are no better in God's sight than the people they employ.

All of this, everything from verse one to verse nine, is so contrary to human nature. But God does not expect the natural from those He has redeemed; He expects the supernatural, and He provides His Word and the Holy Spirit to make it a reality in our lives.

Chapter Eighteen

Armor Up

Ephesians 6:10 *Finally, my brethren, be strong in the Lord, and in the power of his might.* **11** *Put on the whole armour of God, that ye may be able to stand against the wiles of the devil.* **12** *For we wrestle not against flesh and blood, but against principalities, against powers, against the rulers of the darkness of this world, against spiritual wickedness in high places.* **13** *Wherefore take unto you the whole armour of God, that ye may be able to withstand in the evil day, and having done all, to stand.* **14** *Stand therefore, having your loins girt about with truth, and having on the breastplate of righteousness;* **15** *And your feet shod with the preparation of the gospel of peace;* **16** *Above all, taking the shield of faith, wherewith ye shall be able to quench all the fiery darts of the wicked.* **17** *And take the helmet of salvation, and the sword of the Spirit, which is the word of God:* **18** *Praying always with all prayer and supplication in the Spirit, and watching thereunto with all perseverance and supplication for all saints;*

Every letter must finally have a "finally," and Ephesians now does. Paul spent three chapters laying the spiritual foundation of his letter to the Ephesians and then went on in the second half of the letter to spell out the practical outgrowth that is to follow from that foundation. Simply put, since God has been so very gracious to allow us into the household of faith, since He has, in fact, predestined us Gentiles to this high honor from eternity past, we surely ought to gladly live for Him here and now. And the last specific thing he taught concerning that was the obedience and gentleness expected in regard to children, fathers, servants, and masters.

And now, knowing his letter is drawing to a close, and knowing the devil will never leave them alone, Paul will turn his attention to equipping his beloved Ephesian believers to withstand any and all of his assaults.

Our strength

Ephesians 6:10 *Finally, my brethren, be strong in the Lord, and in the power of his might.*

It is lovely beyond measure that, writing to a primarily Gentile audience of believers, Paul, the Jew, calls them "my brethren." God did a work in Paul's heart that needs to be done in every believer's heart, a work of removing any racism and replacing it with the awareness of the fact that we believers are the family of God.

And to this family Paul gave an imperative command here, *"be strong in the Lord, and in the power of his might."* If those terms sound redundant, understand that, to a large measure, they are. Paul was being repetitive to drive home the fact that our strength as believers does not come from our flesh but from Christ. The more we lean on ourselves, the weaker we will be in the spiritual battle; the more we lean on Him, the stronger we will be in the spiritual battle.

An eighty-year-old grandmother facing the devil in the Lord's power will be more successful than a thirty-year-old power lifter facing the devil in his own power.

Our suit

Ephesians 6:11 *Put on the whole armour of God, that ye may be able to stand against the wiles of the devil.*

When Paul said the words "put on," he said it in such a way as to indicate, "Right now, without any delay, put this on." This was a serious enough issue that he knew they could not afford to dilly-dally! And what they were to put on then, what we are to put on now, is the whole armor of God. We are not to pick and choose; God knows the enemy better than we do and wants to equip us accordingly.

What we are to be standing against, once we are armored up, is "the wiles of the devil." Wiles is from the word *methodias,* and we get our English word "methods" from it. It means wiles, trickery, craft, and deceit. And Paul wrote this four thousand years after the Garden of Eden! You would think that the devil would "update his methods" after four millennia, but since deceit has not stopped working, he has found no need to change. Even in our day, six thousand years after Eden, deceit is still his primary methodology.

Not possession, not oppression, not manifestation, deceit.

Ephesians 6:12 *For we wrestle not against flesh and blood, but against principalities, against powers, against the rulers of the darkness of this world, against spiritual wickedness in high places.*

It was flesh and blood people who crucified Christ, stoned Stephen, beheaded James, stoned Paul, and would later boil John in oil. And yet, Paul said that we are to be strong in the Lord and put on the whole armor of God because we do not wrestle against flesh and blood, but against principalities, against powers, against the rulers of the darkness of this world, against spiritual wickedness in high places.

There are some words to take particular note of in this passage. Wrestle is from the word *palay,* and it indicates a contest in which the goal is to pin one's opponent with one's hand on his neck. It was total subjugation. This spiritual contest that we are in is not a "hand-slapping contest." It is a neck-pinning contest; it is a battle for absolute supremacy.

The second word to take note of is, once again, that tiny conjunction "but." It is once again from *alla*, indicating an extreme contrast. We do not wrestle against flesh and blood, BUT against principalities, against powers, against the rulers of the darkness of this world, against spiritual wickedness in high places. Paul really wanted to drive home the fact that though all we see in this battle is flesh and blood, that is just the front for the real enemy, all of which is spiritual in nature, not fleshly.

So, what specifically are we wrestling against? We are wrestling against demonic powers of four classes or orders.

Principalities is from the word *arkas,* and it means "that which is first." These seem to be the highest order of demonic powers, Satan and those directly around him.

Powers is from the word *exousias,* and it means "authority." It is the same word used in John 1:12 when we are told that Christ has given us "power" to become the sons of God. These powers, authorities in Ephesians 6:12, seem to be those of the second order, those that answer to the devil and those directly around him. You could think of the first order as a king and his princes in the palace, and those of the second order somewhat like regional lords answerable to the throne.

The rulers (of the darkness of this world) is from the word *kosmokratoras,* and we get our word "cosmos" out of that root word. All of it together indicates those who, rather than being in the throne room or directly reporting to the throne room, are tasked with overseeing the day-to-day wickedness and darkness of specific regions and nations of earth.

Spiritual wickedness in high places is pretty interesting. Many people take it to mean in heavenly places, meaning out there in the atmosphere since Satan is the prince of the power of the air. But that does not fit with the pattern we are observing. What does fit is to regard these "high places" as any place of influence over the lives of others, places like schools, libraries, entertainment, sports, work, banking, the military, and much more. And if you are at all paying attention, you know that all of those influential places have seemingly lost their minds recently and are all but openly waving the devil's banner for all the world to see. Demonic powers would just as soon have the local library or your kids' school as anything else on earth because that is where future generations can be warped and twisted into something usable in his filthy hands. And while this is clearly the lowest station of the four classes of demonic powers we face, it is also likely the most influential on a day-by-day basis.

And what are we to be doing in regard to all of this? Wrestling. Fighting back. Attempting to subjugate them like they are attempting to subjugate us. They are not going to "get along with us" at all, ever, so we should feel the exact same way about them.

Ephesians 6:13 *Wherefore take unto you the whole armour of God, that ye may be able to withstand in the evil day, and having done all, to stand.*

This is now the second time in just three verses that Paul has used the phrase "the whole armor of God." He really does want to emphasize that we must not leave any of it off!

He begins with "wherefore." Wherefore, because of all of these demonic powers we wrestle with, take the whole armor of God. The purpose of this is *"that ye may be able to withstand in the evil day, and having done all, to stand."*

"Withstand" and "stand" are two crucial words. Just like you see "stand" in both words, there is a common root in the words they both come from, the word *istaymi*. That is the word for "stand." But in the first word, withstand, the prefix *anthi*, anti, in our vernacular, is added to it. So we have a two-part command that we stand against, and that we stand.

The evil day can be any day; the devil is not too particular about that. Whatever day he thinks he can win against you, he will try. When he does, you must withstand him, you must "stand against" him. Rolling over and playing dead is not an option.

"Having done all" is a military term, and it means "having conquered, having accomplished the goal." Having done all, have stood against the devil and won, "stand." In other words, do not win and then quit. Do not win and then lay the armor down. Win, and then keep the armor on and keep standing because the devil never regards any defeat as final. If he got kicked out of heaven once and then will storm heaven yet again during the Tribulation Period, you may know for a certainty that he will never stop attacking you either.

Ephesians 6:14 *Stand therefore, having your loins girt about with truth, and having on the breastplate of righteousness;*

Verse thirteen ended with stand, and verse fourteen begins with the same word from the same root. Paul was pretty serious about us continuing to stand and always standing!

We are commanded here to stand, *"having your loins girt about with truth."* This, the covering of the loins, is the first part of our spiritual armor. The girt, or "girdle," spoken of here was a belt, often made of metal, which held all of the various pieces of the armor together and on which the sword hung. Without it, a soldier could never really have armor, just a bunch of loose pieces that did not stick to him.

This girdle, this belt, is truth. Truth is to hold everything together for us. Without having truth as our "cinch belt" on a daily basis, we are in deep trouble.

None of us could have imagined thirty years ago that we would be watching anyone at all say foolish things like, "If he says he is a woman, he is a woman!" And yet, it is now not just drug-addled addicts saying such patently untrue things; it is even many "preachers" that are saying it! The devil has taken the most obvious truth in the entire universe, something that six thousand years of humanity, saved and lost alike, universally agreed upon, and made it into a raging debate.

All of the powers of darkness are laughing at us.

A lot of Christians laid down the belt of truth in other areas, areas that made their children angry or caused them issues at work, and now nothing is off limits. There will come a day when people in high places are saying, "Christians are actually already dead, so feel free to kill them," and the world will believe it and do it all the while you are saying, "I'm not dead, I am right here in front of you very much alive!"

Every single day, the first thing you better put on by way of armor is truth; it is what ties everything else together.

The second part of the armor is the breastplate of righteousness. The breastplate is what covered the body from the neck all the way down to the thighs both in front and in back. It covers all of the vital organs; it is that which is most likely to keep you from dying in combat.

There are two aspects to righteousness, and only one is spoken of here, so we need to know which is which. There is the positional righteousness we are granted in Christ the moment we believe, and there is the practical righteousness of daily life that is to flow from that positional righteousness.

We do not have the ability to "put on" our positional righteousness; that is a once-and-forever gift granted to us upon salvation. The righteousness spoken of here, then, is the day-by-day practical kind of righteousness.

It is, in other words, "right doing."

And it should not take a professional theologian to see the myriad of ways this keeps us alive in this spiritual battle.

One of the strongest, straightest, most sought-after preachers of our day laid aside this breastplate of righteousness, right doing, and had sex with a prostitute. His "positional righteousness" did not protect him; he lost everything that matters short of salvation itself and would give anything to get it back.

One of the best singers of our day, a lady that girls everywhere looked up to, bolted from home and went to live in sin with another man. Her "positional righteousness" did not protect her; she lost everything that matters short of salvation itself and would give anything to get it back.

Another solid and effective preacher started dabbling in drugs. He ended up in prison and later took his own life. His "positional righteousness" did not protect him; he lost everything that matters short of salvation itself and, finally, his own life.

Another pretty well-known preacher developed a pornography habit. It got so bad that he was watching it in his office in the church. And yet he was so "super-pious" about his positional righteousness in Christ that he legitimately believed God would do nothing since "Jesus paid it all." As it turns out, that was not the case, and when everything came out, he lost his wife, his kids, his ministry, and his reputation.

We, as Christians, often far underestimate this matter of practical, daily righteousness. If you will not do right, you are leaving yourself open for fatal blows from the devil.

Ephesians 6:15 *And your feet shod with the preparation of the gospel of peace;*

We may be tempted to look at the armor of God and then get to this point in the list and say, "Shoes? Seriously?" But anyone who thinks that knows nothing of the history of war.

On December 23, 1777, in the midst of the Revolutionary War, George Washington wrote these words in a letter to Henry Laurens, the President of the Continental Congress:

> "A number of men [remain] confined to hospitals for want of shoes, and others in farmer's houses on the

same account. We have by a field return this day made, no less than 2898 men now in camp unfit for duty because they are barefoot and otherwise naked."

That was nearly one-quarter of Washington's army.

(US Department)

Without proper shoes, soldiers can neither advance nor even stand their ground. You can have the best weapon in the world, but if you are barefoot and bleeding from your feet, you are going to lose.

The shoes in our spiritual armor, which, by the way, usually covered to just below the knee, are *"the preparation of the gospel of peace."* In other words, being daily prepared to share the gospel with others.

How is that part of our armor? How does being ready at any moment to share the gospel protect us and help us to advance/stand our ground as needed?

The realization that souls are dying and going to hell and have no hope to escape that fate if we do not reach them with the gospel gives us the "traction" we need to stand and to advance. We as believers do not have "ballerina feet;" we have battle feet, and the battlefield is the souls of men.

Ephesians 6:16 *Above all, taking the shield of faith, wherewith ye shall be able to quench all the fiery darts of the wicked.*

When you consider how important all of the rest of the armor is (after all, who wants to be scrambling for loose parts without the belt, or impaled for lack of the breastplate, or smack a pinky-toe on the devil's coffee table for lack of shoes?), it makes the words "above all" pretty dramatic words. Above all else, take the shield of faith.

The type of shield spoken of here was the larger type of shield, the scutum, and was generally about two and a half feet wide and four feet high. It was often covered in treated leather, sometimes in metal, and it, especially the one covered in metal, literally did help to protect against fiery arrows.

"The wicked" is used here as a title and designation for the devil. The devil does not just want to skewer you; he wants to burn you to the ground. The good news is a very specific shield, the shield of faith, will prevent that. If you maintain your confidence in God for all of the issues of your everyday life, the devil will never burn you down. It is when we allow him to sow doubts in our hearts about God's care for us that we drop that shield and make ourselves vulnerable to his fiery darts.

Ephesians 6:17 *And take the helmet of salvation, and the sword of the Spirit, which is the word of God:*

Up until this point, the Ephesians may have been getting nervous; nothing had been said thus far about protecting the head, one of the most vulnerable points in any battle. Paul gets to that in this verse, though, reminding them to wear the helmet of salvation. And it is evident that he was not speaking of their need to be saved – he had already called them brethren. He was telling them, in so many words, to "cover their brain with that truth."

How many truly saved people has the devil ruined by constantly sowing doubts about their salvation?

It is interesting that those who are seemingly very clearly lost (shacking up, drinking, never go to church, curse like sailors) never seem to doubt their "salvation," while people who live for the Lord with every fiber of their being and are faithful and serve the Lord are constantly beset by doubts.

The devil is pretty good at what he does.

Put on the helmet of salvation. That thing that God did in your heart? Cover your head with it. Learn the doctrine of salvation thoroughly. Memorize all of the verses. Thank God for your salvation every single time you pray. Take up the helmet of salvation!

Lastly, Paul instructs that we are to take *"the sword of the Spirit, which is the word of God:"*

This is the only offensive piece of the armor.

It is also the only one we need.

What God said (which He, by the way, has been so kind as to put into a book for us) is our weapon. And it is a weapon that even Jesus, the omnipotent Son of God, used. When He faced off against the devil Himself, He three times quoted from the book of Deuteronomy. If Jesus would not face the devil without the Word, what makes any of us think that we should do so?

I know, I know, you have heard people "Bind the devil and cast him out." Stupid is pretty cheap these days, so some people tend to stock up on it.

The only weapon you have against the devil is the word "In" found in Genesis 1:1 and the word "amen" found in Revelation 22:21, and the other 783,135 words in between that in and that amen. If you do not actually know your Bible, then you really do not have a sword at all.

Our supplication

Ephesians 6:18 *Praying always with all prayer and supplication in the Spirit, and watching thereunto with all perseverance and supplication for all saints;*

So, you have your armor. What are you to do now, go out looking for the devil?

No. You are to be *"Praying always with all prayer and supplication in the Spirit, and watching thereunto with all perseverance and supplication for all saints."*

Praying always. Never letting up. Opening your day with prayer, closing your day with prayer, and being in a constant running conversation with God between those two points.

Praying always with all prayer seems a bit redundant, but really is not. It basically means "praying with all kinds of prayer." Pray things like the Lord's prayer. Pray over your meals. Lead in prayer in church. Whatever "kind of prayer" is called for at any given moment, pray that prayer.

But pray with supplication also. Supplication means "asking for what you need." Never give in to the Pious Pierre's and Grim Gloria's who lecture, "Do not come to God with your list of needs; come to God with your list of thanks."

If I am drowning, I am praying for a lifeboat, not thanking God for the lungs that are now filling up with water.

The next phrase, *"watching thereunto with all perseverance,"* means "watching for opportunities to pray and never giving up on it." Prayer is to be something we look for reasons to do, not merely something we check off of our list of duties each day.

Lastly, we find the phrase *"and supplication for all saints."* Just like we pray for our own needs, we are to likewise pray for the needs of all of our other family in Christ. Believers should be able to know that whatever they are going through, believers everywhere are praying for them.

All of this is part of our "finally," part of the things Paul wanted to leave us with as he began to bring this letter to a close. Stand, suit up, and make supplication for yourself and others.

Chapter Nineteen
No Time for Timidity

Ephesians 6:19 *And for me, that utterance may be given unto me, that I may open my mouth boldly, to make known the mystery of the gospel,* **20** *For which I am an ambassador in bonds: that therein I may speak boldly, as I ought to speak.* **21** *But that ye also may know my affairs, and how I do, Tychicus, a beloved brother and faithful minister in the Lord, shall make known to you all things:* **22** *Whom I have sent unto you for the same purpose, that ye might know our affairs, and that he might comfort your hearts.* **23** *Peace be to the brethren, and love with faith, from God the Father and the Lord Jesus Christ.* **24** *Grace be with all them that love our Lord Jesus Christ in sincerity. Amen. <To the Ephesians written from Rome, by Tychicus.>*

Paul had just finished instructing the Ephesian believers to pray, not just for themselves, but for all of the saints. But as he begins this final section of his letter, he narrows down the scope from "all the saints" to "me." And do not think for a moment he was being self-centered when he did so; both his present circumstance and his precious calling really did need the prayers of the saints.

A surprising request

Ephesians 6:19 *And for me, that utterance may be given unto me, that I may open my mouth boldly, to make known the mystery of the gospel,* **20** *For which I am an ambassador in bonds: that therein I may speak boldly, as I ought to speak.*

There are certain things that, if a person asked you to pray for them, you would probably be surprised about since they seem to have that area covered quite nicely. Think, perhaps, of Fat Albert asking you to pray that he could overcome his anorexia.

As surprising as that prayer request would be, I believe it pales in comparison to Paul asking the Ephesians to pray for him to be able to speak the gospel boldly. When did Paul ever have a problem speaking anything boldly, especially the gospel!

But the phrase that he uses at the very beginning of the verse shows that Paul had a better understanding of the situation than we tend to have:

"And for me, that utterance may be given unto me..."

Utterance is from the rather famous word *logos*. In its most basic sense, it means "a word." If you have ever heard a preacher say, "We need a word from the Lord," he is expressing the exact same saying that Paul is saying here. In other words, Paul was tying him receiving a word from the Lord to give to others to the ability of him to speak with boldness. If all he had was his opinion or his desires or his theories, he knew that he could not rightly speak with boldness. And he wanted to speak with boldness so that, in his own words, he could *"make known the mystery of the gospel."*

When you think of putting the words boldness and mystery in the same context as what we say, Paul's thought process gets pretty clear. As he has made abundantly well known throughout his letters, the gospel was a mystery, it was something that was true from the earliest times but had been hidden and was now being revealed.

If you are going to say something that is not well accepted because people have been saying something different for a very long time, you better be able to do so with boldness. And as children of God, the only way we will ever be able to speak the mystery of the gospel with boldness is if God gives us the words to say.

Segueing off of that word gospel at the end of verse nineteen, Paul says this in the very next verse:

Ephesians 6:20 *For which I am an ambassador in bonds: that therein I may speak boldly, as I ought to speak.*

"*For which*" means "because of which." So think of it this way, "The gospel, because of which I am an ambassador in bonds." Paul was, at that very moment, in chains because he preached the gospel. He was a prisoner because of his preaching. But the word he uses of himself before he gets to that word bonds is a shocking word. He called himself an *ambassador* in bonds.

From the time of the ancient world up until now in our modern world, ambassadors have been viewed as untouchable; to put one in chains was and is unthinkable to the point of likely even provoking a war if it happens. An ambassador speaks for a nation; imprison the ambassador, and you have done a grave injustice to the entire populace.

But Paul was not just any ambassador; he was an ambassador of the King of kings, the Lord of Glory. And yet mankind, with the Jews initiating the process and the Romans carrying it out, put God's ambassador in chains.

A person in a circumstance like that could get bewildered and frightened. So, how would Paul handle it? Here was his answer to that:

"*That therein I may speak boldly, as I ought to speak.*"

One thing we need to clear up is what the "therein" refers to. Grammatically, it does not refer to the bonds of verse twenty but back to the ambassadorship of the gospel of verses nineteen and twenty. He was not saying, "Pray that I can speak boldly in my position as a prisoner," he was saying, "Pray that I can speak boldly in my position as an ambassador!" The chains were of far less significance to Paul than the calling.

And that is the way that every one of us should regard it, especially since many of us are likely to end up in bonds as Paul did and for the same reason, given the demonic storm clouds that are gathering across our culture. So if we end up in chains, remember that the calling is more significant than the chains, and pray that we might all have the word from the Lord to speak so that we may have boldness as we declare the gospel to a world that does not want to hear it.

A soothing reply

Ephesians 6:21 *But that ye also may know my affairs, and how I do, Tychicus, a beloved brother and faithful minister in the Lord, shall make known to you all things:* **22** *Whom I have sent unto you for the same purpose, that ye might know our affairs, and that he might comfort your hearts.*

There is something truly beautiful in these verses. The Ephesians had been asking questions because they wanted to know what was going on with Paul and how he was doing! There was a connection between this congregation and this man of God. He did not just love them; they loved him, too. So, because Paul knew that they wanted to know how he was doing, he sent Tychicus in reply to bring them the letter and to fill them in on everything else as well.

Who was this Tychicus?

Here is what Scripture tells us.

Acts 20:4 *And there accompanied him into Asia Sopater of Berea; and of the Thessalonians, Aristarchus and Secundus; and Gaius of Derbe, and Timotheus; and of Asia, Tychicus and Trophimus.*

This is the first passage in Scripture in which we read of Tychicus. Paul has just come through a major uproar in Ephesus; he is now heading towards Macedonia, and the company going with him includes Tychicus of Asia, most likely from right there in Ephesus.

And then we read of him here in Ephesians 6 as a trusted messenger from Paul back to the church at Ephesus.

Colossians 4:7 *All my state shall Tychicus declare unto you, who is a beloved brother, and a faithful minister and fellowservant in the Lord:* **8** *Whom I have sent unto you for the same purpose, that he might know your estate, and comfort your hearts;*

Here yet again, we find Paul speaking of Tychicus in the most glowing of terms, calling him a beloved brother and a faithful minister and a fellow servant in the Lord, and entrusting him with a message to the church at Colosse.

Titus 3:12 *When I shall send Artemas unto thee, or Tychicus, be diligent to come unto me to Nicopolis: for I have determined there to winter.*

Here yet again, we find Tychicus as a trusted messenger for Paul. Unlike so many in the life of Paul, nothing negative is ever said or inferred about Tychicus; each time we are introduced or reintroduced to him in Scripture, he is nothing but a blessing.

Every one of us should strive to be a Tychicus.

A sweet resolution

Ephesians 6:23 *Peace be to the brethren, and love with faith, from God the Father and the Lord Jesus Christ.* **24** *Grace be with all them that love our Lord Jesus Christ in sincerity. Amen. <To the Ephesians written from Rome, by Tychicus.>*

Let me show you these verses again and isolate four words for you to show you how sweet a resolution these closing words from Paul to the Ephesians are:

Ephesians 6:23 ***Peace*** *be to the brethren, and **love** with **faith**, from God the Father and the Lord Jesus Christ.* **24 *Grace*** *be with all them that love our Lord Jesus Christ in sincerity. Amen. <To the Ephesians written from Rome, by Tychicus.>*

Paul was not in the habit of closing letters like this. The vast majority of the time, he simply wishes them grace in his closing words. But the Ephesians were so dear to him that he added a wish for peace and love and faith to go along with the grace for them!

That grace, though, came with a qualifier: *"Grace be with all them that love our Lord Jesus Christ in sincerity. Amen."*

"In sincerity" simply means being genuine about it. Many people claim to love the Lord; some actually do, and you can tell the difference by the way they live their lives. Here is how Jesus himself put it:

John 14:15 *If ye love me, keep my commandments.*

Here is how John the Apostle put it many years after the time of Paul:

1 John 5:3 *For this is the love of God, that we keep his commandments: and his commandments are not grievous.*

Loving Christ sincerely is not wearing a tiny cross around your neck while you parade around nearly naked in public; it is putting your clothes on since God has commanded modesty.

Loving Christ sincerely is not posting inspirational quotes online Sunday morning at about 11 o'clock; it is being in church since God has commanded that we come together to worship.

Loving Christ sincerely is not wearing a WWJD bracelet; it is actively trying to win souls since that is the Great Commission that He gave us.

There are thousands of possible applications here. Simply put, if you sincerely love God, it will be evident because you obey Him. And if you do sincerely love God, in the words of Paul as he closes out this letter, "grace be with you."

Works Cited

Buddemeyer, R., & Chilton, C. (2019, December 12). *60 strict rules the royal family has to follow*. Marie Claire Magazine. https://www.marieclaire.com/culture/g4985/strict-rules-the-royal-family-has-to-follow (Accessed July 8, 2023)

Clarke, A. (1977). *The holy bible, containing the old and new testaments, the text carefully printed from the most correct copies of the present authorized translation, including the marginal readings and parallel texts: With a commentary and critical notes designed as a help to a better understanding of the sacred writings* (Vols. 5-6). Abingdon Press.

Gannett Satellite Information Network. (n.d.). *Rikkie Kollé becomes first transgender woman to win miss netherlands pageant*. USA Today. https://www.usatoday.com/videos/life/2023/07/13/rikkie-kolle-first-transgender-woman-become-miss-netherlands/12249827002 (Accessed July 19, 2023)

Henry, M. (n.d.). *Matthew Henry's commentary on the whole Bible* (Vol. 6). F.H. Revell.

Hobbs, J. (2023, July 6). *I chopped off my finger - now I'm removing skin to look like an alien*. New York Post. https://nypost.com/2023/07/06/i-cut-off-my-finger-now-im-removing-skin-to-look-like-an-alien/ (Accessed July 19/2023)

Jamieson, R., Fausset, A. R., & Brown, D. (1997). *A commentary on the old and new testaments* (Vol. 3). Hendrickson Publishers.

John-Bett. (2021, June 25). *Woman mourns after her dolphin husband dies and says she will never remarry*. The Mirror. https://www.mirror.co.uk/news/weird-news/woman-mourns-after-dolphin-husband-24395652 (Accessed July 19, 2023)

Linder, Phil. Power Bible CD v 5.9, 2010

Qurollo, J. A. (2011). *Notes on Ephesians*. Qurollo Publishing.

Reilly, D. (2023, April 29). *From transgendered to "transabled": People are "choosing" to identify as handicapped*. New York Post. https://nypost.com/2023/04/29/transabled-people-choosing-to-identify-as-handicapped (Accessed July 19, 2023)

U.S. Department of the Interior. (n.d.). *Tracked by their blood upon the Rough Frozen Ground (U.S. National Park Service)*. National Parks Service. http://www.nps.gov/articles/000/valley-forge-footwear-3.htm (Accessed August 12, 2023)

Winnail, D. S. (2017, January 5). *How "Christianity" Changed the World*. Tomorrow's World. https://www.tomorrowsworld.org/magazines/2016/november-december/how-christianity-changed-the-world (Accessed April 21, 2023)

Other Books by Dr. Wagner

Daniel: Breathtaking
Esther: Five Feasts and the Fingerprints of God
Galatians: Treasures of Liberty
James: The Pen and the Plumb Line
Jonah: A Story of Greatness
Nehemiah: A Labor of Love
Proverbs Vol 1: Bright Light from Dark Sayings
Proverbs Vol 2: Bright Light from Dark Sayings
The Revelation: Ready or Not
Romans: Salvation from A-Z
Ruth: Diamonds in the Darkness

Beyond the Colored Coat
From Footers to Finish Nails
Learning Not to Fear the Old Testament
Marriage Makers/Marriage Breakers
I'm Saved! Now What???
Don't Muzzle the Ox

Books in the Night Heroes Series

Cry from the Coal Mine (Vol 1)
Free Fall (Vol 2)
Broken Brotherhood (Vol 3)
The Blade of Black Crow (Vol 4)
Ghost Ship (Vol 5)
When Serpents Rise (Vol 6)
Moth Man (Vol 7)
Runaway (Vol 8)
Terror by Day (Vol 9)
Winter Wolf (Vol 10)
Desert Heat (Vol 11)

Other Fiction

Zak Blue: Falcon Wing
Zak Blue: Enter the Maelstrom

Devotionals

DO Drops Vol. 1
DO Drops Vol. 2
DO Drops Vol. 3
DO Drops Vol. 4
DO Drops Vol. 5
DO Drops Vol. 6
DO Drops Vol. 7
DO Drops Vol. 8
DO Drops Vol. 9
DO Drops Vol 10

www.ingramcontent.com/pod-product-compliance
Lightning Source LLC
LaVergne TN
LVHW051115080426
835510LV00018B/2052